KING
FOR
EVER

KING FOR EVER

JAMES S. STEWART

*"The Lord sat as King at the flood;
yea, the Lord sitteth King for ever."*—THE PSALMIST

ABINGDON

Nashville

KING FOR EVER

ISBN 0-687-20883-1

Two of these studies have already appeared in print, and for permission
to include them here I am grateful to the editors and publishers of
To God Be the Glory: Sermons in Honor of George Arthur Buttrick by
Theodore Gill (Abingdon Press, 1973), and *Best Sermons* ed. Dr. Paul
Butler (Trident Press, 1968).

MANUFACTURED BY THE PARTHENON PRESS AT
NASHVILLE, TENNESSEE, UNITED STATES OF AMERICA

This book is dedicated to
ROBIN and JAN
and
JACK and GRETA

CONTENTS

THE SHOUT OF A KING

"The Lord their God is with them,
and the shout of a king is among them."
NUMBERS 23:21 (RSV)

It is an extraordinary story—this picture of how the king of
Moab tried to destroy the people of Israel by hiring a soothsayer
to curse them. There was the Israelite army in the tents clustered
together on the plain, quite unconscious of the dark conspiracy
that was brewing, and there, on the crags of the heights above,
was this Moabite king called Balak, bandying his hireling prophet
about, hurrying the wretched, breathless Balaam from one point
of vantage to another, urging him to use the black arts of wiz-
ardry and magic and enchantment to spellbind that host en-
camped down beneath them in the sunshine and so bring evil
upon them and blight them and destroy them.

And Balaam looked on the tents of Israel and shook his head
and said, "No, Balak, you may be monarch of Moab, and you
may have paid me well, but I cannot do it. I cannot curse what
God has blessed."

But the superstitious king persisted. "You must and shall do
it! Try again. Come, we shall go to yonder hilltop across the
valley. You will not see the whole imposing array of Israel from
that point—only a part of it. That will make your sorcery easier,
and you will curse Israel for me from there!"

And so he badgered the luckless prophet, but always the evil
plan was thwarted, always came the same infuriating answer, "I
cannot do it! King or no king, bribe or no bribe, I cannot curse
what God has blessed. There is no necromancy ever invented that
can reverse the divine decree. Not by one jot or tittle can I change

it, not for all the gold and silver you can offer me." And Balaam looked again at Israel camped down there beneath them and spoke to the angry man beside him, "I tell you, Balak, prince of Moab, there is no spell, no magic malediction in the world, that will bind or shackle that host. For the Lord their God is with them, and the shout of a king is among them."

There, then, is the story. Now we are going to leave it behind and concentrate on that final word. It was indeed a magnificent tribute to the presence of the Spirit of God in Israel, all the more remarkable for being forced and reluctant and unwilling. What we have to ask ourselves now is the question: Is it still true? Is it true of the second Israel, the new Israel, which is the church of Jesus Christ?

Let us take the two assertions separately. The first is a declaration of *the divine presence. "The Lord their God is with them."*

Historically it is a fact that what made the original Israel, the Israel of the desert and the promised land, was the presence of God in the midst. What constituted them a community and a marching army and eventually a nation was not their legal system nor their genius for colonizing, not impressive numbers nor expert leadership; it was this thing which Balaam had stumbled against unwittingly, as against a rock of granite. "The Lord their God is with them." As long as that was there, Israel was invincible. When that went, everything went. When that collapsed, Israel's banners were trailed in dust.

So, too, historically it is a fact that what has made the second Israel, the church of the Christian centuries, has been precisely that. Not influential patronage, not apostolic succession, not the democratic vote of General Assemblies, not even confessional orthodoxy, but this one thing—the vitality of the Spirit, the adoring awareness of a supernatural environment, the presence of God in the midst. "The Lord their God is with them!" As long as that is there, the heart of the church's worship and witness and work is sound. But when that goes, everything goes. When that is lost, all we can bring in to fill the gap is worth exactly nothing.

How would you suggest filling such a vacuum? Venerable church tradition and efficient organization? Elaborate care for structure and fabric and institution? Prayers in contemporary language, ritual and liturgy updated, brighter music, zeal of humanitarian and social endeavor, politics in the pulpit? Perhaps even a gentle toning down of the uncompromising note of finality and uniqueness which characterizes the Christian revelation, to accommodate it to the temper of a pluralist society? All vain and shallow, if God is not there in the midst; all just tinkering with the problem, apart from the Spirit of the Lord.

And I wonder—when our twentieth-century Balaams encounter Israel now, when the world comes up against the church today—is there anything of that compunction which smote Balaam to the soul, the feeling "I cannot do anything! There is something here right out of this world, mysterious, transcendent, supernatural. The Lord their God is with them"? Do they feel that? Or rather—for this is the real question—whether they feel it or not, is that a fact? .

This is the most urgent question the church can ever ask itself. For all around us today there are multitudes restless and dissatisfied and groping and hungry, and they do not know what they are groping for; that rebellious dissatisfaction is driving some of them, specially the younger ones among them, to experiment with all kinds of queer cults that are apt to puzzle and perhaps shock their elders. They do not know what that inner craving is, and they would probably laugh if you suggested it had anything to do with traditional religion. But in its own strange way it is indeed a hunger for some real bread of life; it is the longing of the exile to get his head above the suffocating vapors of the world's materialism and to breathe his native air. It is the need for something to worship, someone to adore. It is precisely the psalmist's quest, "My heart and my flesh cry out for the living God!" Now tell me—given that situation, what is the use of a church that is not throbbing with God's own life, vibrant with the dimension of the supernatural?

It is a desolating thing to go through a church service in which no vivid sense of the transcendent is apparent, no opening of the windows toward an unseen reality, no gleam of supernatural light streaming through from the eternal world.

The fact is, it is this transcendent thing, this stretching of the horizons to unseen realities, this immersion in the Spirit—it is this alone which can make us a church, and not just a benevolent club or one more redundant society. "The Lord their God is with them"—this holds the answer to the need of all mankind, good news for dying men, not good advice. This and this alone can bring deliverance from all the fatalism, futility, and disillusionment that are corrupting our world today.

Think of that kind of church. How quickened its worship! How alive and real and filled with awe and gratitude and adoration! And how deepened its fellowship! "The Lord their God is with them": that does not level out our idiosyncrasies or cancel our different points of view, but it does make us members of a great family, and everyone around us a brother for whom Christ died. And how energized its evangelism! What a new passion to get involved in the world and to share with others that life of God for lack of which the world is dying! "You are a colony of heaven," Paul told the church at Philippi, and that is indeed the vivid, bracing truth: a colony of heaven, God's embassy to implement his redemptive purpose here on earth, Christ's hands and feet to carry into the world's life the love he died to reveal and the spiritual power he lives for ever to impart. In every aspect of the church's life, the divine presence is the one thing that matters. May it always be said of those who worship here, "The Lord their God is with them."

That was the one side of Balaam's declaration. Turn now to the other. Balaam stood there looking down on the tents of Israel in the valley, this host he had been bribed to ruin. "No," he said to Balak, "I cannot do it. No spellbinder or necromancer in the world could do it. For the Lord their God is with them." And then suddenly he added this lightning word, *"And the shout of a king is among them."*

Is that not magnificently apposite for the new Israel, the

church? First, the presence of God, and now, *the victory of Christ.*

Who that knows the story of the new Israel, whose king and head is Christ, has not heard some echo of that shout reverberating across the centuries? Always it has kept breaking out anew in the great triumphant days when a Francis, a Luther, a Wesley have given the church back its soul, always that ringing joyful confidence, like the chant of a marching host, always that shout of a king!

"Well," you say, "it does not seem to me that there is very much of that in the church today. It seems to me that any such resounding triumphant conviction is conspicuous by its absence." And then you go on to diagnose the dilemma. You say, "There is this mounting crisis of belief of which we hear so much, hanging like a miasma over the church's life and witness. There are the discouraging statistics providing ample material for every self-appointed prophet of pessimism and gloom. There are all the contemporary bewilderments and uncertainties, the haunting doubt about relevance and reality, the feeling that perhaps we had better wait a hundred or a thousand years till a new age of faith is born, and in the meantime the less said the better about the possibility of saving a secular society. Not much of the shout of a king there!"

If that is true—and I am not denying that there is an element of truth in such a diagnosis—it is because we have been allowing the magnitude of our problems to blind us to the majesty of our Master. Why can we not see that, massive as our contemporary problems are, God's mighty act in Christ is infinitely greater? Why do we persist in living as if "Immanuel, God with us" were some sort of psychological self-suggestion or rhetorical mysticism, and not—as indeed it is—the most exciting and irrefragable of facts? Why are we not glorying in the Lord?

But there is also a different kind of attitude current today, equally mistaken. There is the attitude that frowns on anything like what it calls "triumphalism" in religion. It has no desire, it will tell you, to hear in its religion the shout of a king. Anything savoring of triumphalism—from the confident and unabashed assertion of a once-for-all salvation, universally valid for ever, down to much lesser things, down even to the ordered dignity of a church procession, or a General Assembly's psalm-singing that makes the rafters ring—it labels an offense. It maintains that the really radical thing about Christianity is not the shout of a King but the cry of dereliction. It tells us that Jesus was not a scepter-bearing monarch but the "man for others," not the conqueror renowned but the servant girt with a towel washing men's feet, and that therefore Christianity must soft-pedal its victory songs and tone down its soul-winning glad heroics and mute or stop its rhapsodizing about invincible world salvation. Instead of that, let it get on and be practical, with the humbler duties of secular involvement and political, economic, and social humanitarianism.

There is just enough truth in this half-truth to make it dangerously misleading. It is nowhere near measuring up to the full-orbed truth of the New Testament. Certainly the apostles are not above using triumphal language when they talk of Christ. "Every day I live," cried Paul to the Corinthians, "he leads me in triumph in his victory march." "In the world you shall have tribulation," said Jesus, "but I have overcome the world." If we cannot hear the shout of a King in that—that "I have overcome," so much more radical than the song of the modern revolutionary "We will overcome"—we must be deaf indeed.

It was on Calvary itself, we are told, that the royal shout first startled the world, shattering and remaking history. Jesus uttered a loud cry—with his dying breath it came, a conqueror's shout—"It is finished!" And that meant, "The decisive battle is finished. Death and darkness and the devil are irrevocably defeated for ever!" Our Christian faith is that in that moment of victory the whole human prospect was changed. At that point in history there was a new creation, the daybreak of the world. And the ratification was the resurrection. In one irreducibly miraculous act, baffling all natural explanation, God raised him on high, and gave him a name above every name. And the early church took up the shout. "Christ reigns!" shouted the martyrs at the stake and went down into the darkness shouting it and passed, shouting to the throne of God.

But, beware of triumphalism, we are told. I answer now, Why should we not be triumphal? It is indeed true that Christ is the servant Messiah, the "man for others." But it is also true that God has given him the kingdom and the cosmic dominion, and on his head are many crowns. What we need to do is not so much to possess this revealed truth as to be possessed by it—the absolute finality of Christus Victor, Christ triumphant.

Of course, it is right that as Christians we should agonize over the plight of the "third world," the miseries of men and nations victimized by war and famine, poverty and discrimination and injustice; right that we should be devising ways and means of revolutionizing and remedying the hateful conscience-searing iniquities; right that by all means in our power we should be serving the suffering and the downtrodden and the oppressed, and doing it in the name of Christ. But it is wrong if that agonizing and that revolutionizing and that serving rob us of the note of victory. It is all wrong if we yield to the suggestion that with the world as it is there is something not quite decent in Christian worship striking the note of unalloyed triumphant gladness.

The world's dark night may still continue pressing in upon us, but if I have seen Christ, then I know that the darkness of history is now shot through with unquenchable hope and with the final certainty of the glorious outcome of all its struggles. Or make it more personal. I may go down into the dark, but if I do, I am still in the hands of him who bears the scepter of all the universes and everlastingly makes all things new, here and hereafter, and therefore I am safe for ever.

I am not minimizing the trouble of the world or of the individual. I should be a fool to play down the vastness of our world rehabilitation task or the length of the campaign. What I am saying is that, if there had been no Christ going before conquering and to conquer, the task would have been hopeless and the campaign disastrous. It is precisely because Christ has overcome once and for all that we can see the end of the road in sight and know that the future is secure. This is the fact that cannot be shaken. This is the rock of God beneath our feet. Let us not be abashed by the criticism of triumphalism. We are indeed triumphing in Christ. The Lord our God is with us. The shout of a King is among us.

How I wish I could help someone to hear it today! To hear it not only in our worship service and in our world crusade, but in the interior experiences of your own soul. To know that, whatever life may do to you, you can and shall—through the victory of Christ—be more than conqueror. To know that your life, every day you live, has a background, and that the background is nothing less than God's victory in Christ over every possible foe that can ever assail you.

Of course, all this is miracle—sheer miracle. But it is happening every day in the lives of thousands. And why not for you? Why not for you?

"The Lord their God is with them, and the shout of a King is among them." God grant we may hear it now and believe it—that ringing and reverberating shout of Christ athwart the ages—and may joyfully yield to him our heart's allegiance.

TO GOD BE THE GLORY!

"We have this treasure in earthen vessels,
to show that the transcendent power belongs to God and not to us."
2 CORINTHIANS 4:7 (RSV)

Here is a contrast of the most dramatic kind, a stark, bewildering incongruity and disproportion. Treasure—in earthen vessels. It is not fitting that anyone should enclose a lovely picture in a tawdry frame or a priceless jewel in a flimsy box of cardboard or a royal diadem in a cracked and dingy case in a museum thick with dust. That would clearly be all wrong. Yet this, Paul sees, is precisely what God has done.

There is the startling contrast: on the one side, the magnificence of divine grace, on the other, the worthlessness of the human hearts in which that grace is lodged; such an immense and shining splendor entrusted to such poor, pathetic, broken instruments; such an infallible truth committed to very fallible men; such an amazing gospel committed to such an ordinary church. "We have this treasure in earthen vessels." It is so frightfully incongruous; in fact, it is all wrong! Yet it is God's doing, and so somehow it must be right.

Somewhere there must be a reason and a purpose for the shattering discrepancy. And Paul searches for that purpose—until suddenly it breaks upon him, luminous and incontrovertible. There is indeed a purpose, and it is this: to let the world see that Christianity—with all the triumphs of the faith in individual lives, all the victories of the gospel over life and death and disenchantment and the devil, all the onward march of the mission of the church—that Christianity cannot ever be accounted for by anything in man or in his institutions, cannot possibly be explained by any human skill or virtue or prowess or ability; for any such explanation, when you consider the human persons actually involved, is manifestly ludicrous and absurd. Hence it follows that the explanation must be in God. "We have this treasure in earthen vessels, to show that the transcendent power belongs to God and not to us." Therefore—to God be the glory!

Let us look, first, at the two opposing factors in this contrast—the treasure and its common clay container, then at some of the different ways in which men react to the contrast, and finally at the divine purpose that brings such opposites together.

First, *the treasure.* "We have this treasure." That is Paul's valuation. Is it ours? Do we realize that the gospel, the old familiar gospel, is still—even in a world of space travel and electronic brains—prodigious wealth, the most incomparable of blessings? Or do we look at Paul as at a man rhapsodizing and growing rhetorical about very little?

I know at any rate where Paul borrowed this metaphor. He borrowed it direct from Jesus. Jesus spoke about the fascination of the quest for treasure. He spoke of the dealer in precious stones, who spent his life traveling across land and sea to enrich his collection, and how one day in the diamond market he suddenly saw before him the most perfect pearl, wonderful beyond his dreams, and how he went and sold his whole collection to possess himself of that one priceless jewel. That, said Jesus, is what it means to find the kingdom of God.

Do we believe it? Does religion mean anything like that for us?

Just consider. What does our holy faith offer? It comes to one man, miserably aware that he has lost grip and broken faith, perhaps beginning to wonder if life is worth living. It comes to such a one, and it says: "Courage! Here is God's renewal, this very day, for you—the past obliterated!" It comes to a woman, weary and out of heart with drudgery and disappointment, fretfulness and anxiety, and it brings incredible good tidings of tension relaxed and strain vanquished by serenity. It comes to this confused, chaotic, bewildered world, and it tells of the entrance into history of a force of immeasurable range which can literally add on to life a new dimension, transforming the whole human prospect. No wonder the New Testament throbs with excitement from end to end! No wonder Paul clamors and stammers about "unsearchable riches" and "unspeakable gifts." "We have this treasure."

It was this above all else that made Paul himself a missionary. It was this that drove him tirelessly across the earth, leading him to the great uproarious cities of the Orient, Ephesus and Corinth and the rest, with their feverish commercialism and their blatant immoralities—the very name Corinth had given currency to a Greek verb which practically meant "to go to the devil." These were now to be the field for the harvest of Christ. The great frowning mountain ranges of Asia and the hazards of the seas were no barrier to this man, for beyond them were men dying without Christ, and the western winds were full of supplicating voices summoning him to Corinth, Rome, Spain, and the furthest limits of the world. Always there was that driving sense: "I must declare this thing, or die. Necessity is laid upon me; woe is me if I preach not the gospel!"

And to gird the church today for its task of mission and evangelism, what do we need? More modern techniques, no doubt, more up-to-date methods, more contemporary structures of church life, more brand-new machinery. But basically the need is surely this: a far deeper sense of the riches we possess, a far livelier appropriation of the supernatural, transcendent resources that are always present to faith in a Risen Lord. All the springs of missionary power and passion are in these three words, "Jesus, priceless treasure!"

Consider now the other side of the contrast. Turn from the treasure to the container, *the vessel in which it is lodged.*

Take the actual situation here at Corinth. Any discerning citizen of Corinth would have told you that to attempt to launch a new religion into the cosmopolitan secularism of that great cultured and sophisticated city, you would require to have an organization combining something like the wisdom of a Socratic academy and the luster of an Olympic prestige. And instead of that, God chose this strange thing he called his Corinthian church, this heterogeneous handful of converted slaves and artisans, an unimpressive, impossible-looking lot, a mad, preposterous choice to be the spearhead of a new campaign, not worth a second thought in the eyes of those who really mattered, and less than the dust beneath Caesar's chariot wheels. Paul himself had no illusions about them—"not many wise men, not many mighty, not many noble are called"—an odd selection surely for God to work with, poor soiled creatures from the slums of sin, painfully ordinary, often bungling and blundering and breaking down in their allegiance. And this—was it not a colossal, ruinous mistake?—this was the chosen vessel for the treasure of the Lord.

So too, perhaps, in our disconsolate moods we look at the church as it exists today. We see its crippling stupid divisions, its flaws and blunders and complacency, its uninspiring ordinariness. Is this really the instrument for the glory of Christ? Is this "the arm of Christ's strength, the tongue of his Spirit, and the visible token of his presence"?

But Paul's sense of the disparity of things was even more personal than this. He was not looking at that church from the outside. He was looking at himself, less than the least of all God's people in Corinth. In this very letter, he quotes what his fastidious Corinthian critics said about him, "his bodily presence is weak, and his speech contemptible." As much as to say, "We expected someone handsome and godlike, like the athletes of our Isthmian games, someone eloquent and logical, like our supreme masters of rhetoric, but this man, with his insignificant physique and uncouth provincial accent, quite puts us off!"

Such was the incongruity that Corinth saw. But Paul saw an even worse discrepancy, which they had failed to detect. It was not just his handicapped body and broken health that were the earthen vessel, not just the shabby figure and provincial brogue. It was the soul within, the memory-haunted, sin-scarred creature that the flash of Damascus had shown him, on that never-to-be-forgotten day when Jesus had cried, "Saul, Saul, why persecute me? You are crucifying me afresh, putting me to an open shame, crushing the crown of thorns again upon my brow. But now, with my head bleeding and my heart breaking, I have come, Saul, for you, Saul my persecutor, my son!" And the man had come to himself. "Dear Jesus, divine and despised, royal and rejected Jesus! O miserable me!"

So, in some moods, we look at ourselves. Who am I to be the ambassador of this royal Redeemer? To wear the Christian name before the world? To be a sample and a specimen of what the grace of Christ can do? God pity me—poor earthen vessel— utterly unworthy!

Yet precisely this has been the strange, unlikely story of the church across the ages: treasure in earthen vessels.

Now before we go on to look at the divine purpose underlying this startling contrast, notice—for this is very significant —*how men react to this incongruity.* They react in different ways.

One man, for example, wants to have the treasure but to leave the earthen vessel. "Give me religion, but not the church! Why should I not develop my own spiritual life and be a perfectly good Christian, without all this stuffiness of an organized society, all the jarring imperfections of an institution with whose defects I have no sympathy and for whose fellowship I feel no need?" So this man, despising the blundering ineptitudes of the human element, stands aloof from the visible church. And so he scorns the thing for which Christ thought it worthwhile to die.

Another man reacts differently. He is so conscious of the earthiness of the vessel that he refuses to believe in the existence of any treasure. "What is the use of talking," he asks, "about unsearchable riches and incalculable resources? That is plainly sham and sophistry and delusion. For can't you see that God, if there were a God, would have been bound to give some more convincing and impressive demonstration of his existence than this thing you point to, this pathetic minority movement you call the church? If there were really a living Christ, conquering and to conquer, how could the world be such a shameful shambles still? Don't ask me to believe in your treasure when you have nothing but an earthen vessel to display. Unsearchable riches? Yes, unsearchable indeed—because they don't exist!" So this second man scathingly reacts and flings off from religion into skepticism.

A third man acts differently again. He sees the disproportion between the treasure and the vessel, and being a well-meaning Christian, his aim is to reduce the disproportion, to narrow the gap. In other words, he says, "Let us make a vessel that will not be earthy, a container to be worthy of the treasure. Let us produce a church so efficacious that it will represent Christ adequately, strong enough to be equal to its task, confident enough to be commensurate with its world commission. Rise up, and make her great!"

Now far be it from me to decry strength and efficiency in religion. After all, there is no special grace in feebleness and no spiritual beatitude for incompetence and muddle.

But—and this is the point—the danger is that we should put our trust in prowess and efficiency, as though the church were to be sufficient for God rather than that God should be sufficient for the church. For when we do that, however mistakenly well-meaning it may be, it is just as if we turned out the light and cut off the church's true power at its source.

The Pharisee in the temple was a very model of religious strength and efficiency, his religion was really most impressive. But the true church was not there, in that man's bold, brash confidence before God. It was in the uneasy conscience and stammering contrition of the publican, who bowed his head and repented in dust and ashes.

The fact we have to recognize and reckon with is that the church's strength is never going to be equal to the task. Thank God for that: the very fact that there is such a frightening disparity is the hidden secret of the church's power. God forbid we should be misled by the naïve and callow supposition that when the church becomes great and imposing the kingdom of heaven

is coming near. You have only to read history to know that that
is not true. If God's kingdom is not of this world, then a self-
sufficient church would be the ultimate blasphemy.

Men once thought they could erect a church so imposing
that its top would reach to heaven, but God flung down that
tower of Babel and scattered across the earth those who had
tried to build it. And perhaps even today we still need to hear
Jeremiah's cry, "Take away her battlements, for they are not the
Lord's!"

But now look at this. There is a fourth attitude, different from
all these. And this is where our text resolves the paradox. There
is another attitude: *to recognize a divine purpose in the disparity
between the treasure and the vessel. The incongruity is intended.*
The treasure has been put into an earthen vessel, not by mistake, not because nothing better was available. It has been put
there deliberately, by preference, of set purpose. It is upon
human weakness, not human strength, that God chooses to build
his kingdom.

When D. L. Moody first went to Birmingham, that great
Nonconformist leader Dr. R. W. Dale of Carr's Lane Church
went to the mission meetings night after night, watching with
critical eye the methods and mannerisms of this new missioner.
Eventually he went to the evangelist and said, "Moody, I have
seen this mission of yours, and have come to the conclusion that
it is truly of God. I'll tell you why. It is because I can see no
possible relation between you personally and the results your
mission is achieving. Therefore, it must be of God." Very frank
—but very true!

Is it not a great thing to know that God can use us, not merely
in spite of our disqualifying infirmities, but precisely because of
them? Yes, and that God can use the church best when it stops
aiming at prosperity and prestige, stops being infected by the
world's ideas of what constitutes greatness and success, stops
wanting to be strong, as the world counts strength, and hoping
to use that strength to build a kingdom for Christ, that God
can use the church best when by a great act of faith it will offer

to him precisely its weakness, its ordinances, its utter help-lessness, saying, "Lord, take this earthen vessel and let the world see that all the excellency of the power is of thee, and not of us"?

I confess that the more I think of this the more it thrills me. We are so apt to say dejectedly, "God can't use me: that is obvious. I am not clever enough, not spiritual enough. There are days when my heart is as cold and dead as a stone. Lord, get someone else!" And so we settle down in inertia and futility. But if this word of the Lord is true, you must never say that. For—do you not see?—what you feel to be your weakness can be for God's purpose your truest strength. Certainly it is only this that makes the Christian ministry possible. Do you think that I, or the next man, or anyone, would dare to stand in a pulpit and try to speak about the meaning of the world and life and death and eternity, if it were not for one thing, namely, that God has promised to make his presence known through the most broken, stumbling words? And that applies not only to the ministry: it applies equally across the whole range of Christian life. It is precisely our felt weakness and self-dis-trust and baffling inhibitions, our feeling—"Who am I to bear the Christian name before men?" precisely this to which the promise of creative grace is given, "to show that the transcendent power belongs to God and not to us."

I repeat—this ought to thrill you. For you must see that, if this is true, then the church that believes it can be irresistible anywhere, and the individual Christian who understands it is undefeatable. You obviously cannot defeat a man who takes his very weakness and, at God's own request, offers that to be God's weapon. There is no answer to that strategy. It is invin-cible.

This Corinthian church ought, humanly speaking, to have been in a chronic state of gloom and depression—"offscourings of the earth," they were called. Yet just because of that, it rang with triumph. To God be the glory!

And if one day I am feeling at the end of my tether, dis-appointed and defeated and terribly unlike the Christ who has commissioned me to be his witness, then that very experience, by emptying me of self, gives God a chance to fill me and lays me open to resources which in my strongest hours I could never have developed. In fact, it is when you have sunk right down to rock bottom that you suddenly find you have struck the Rock of Ages. And then men begin to take knowledge of you that you have been with Jesus.

What, then, are we to say to these things? It does not matter how poor and unworthy you feel yourself to be, how dreadfully earthen the vessel, as long as you have the treasure. This is the question I leave with you now, as I would leave it with my own soul. Do we have it? And if not, will we ask for it? "How much more will your heavenly Father give the Holy Spirit to them who ask him?" Is our faith a belief in a vague abstraction called "a Christian life"—or is it the living treasure, a sure hold on an unchanging reality away beyond this changing world, a passionate adherence to Jesus and an endless gratitude?

May the dear Savior of us all, risen and alive and most certainly here at this moment, do this great thing in us and for us. The blessing shall be ours—and to God be the glory!

A VOICE
OUT OF THE CONGREGATION

*"Now therefore are we all here present before God,
to hear all things that are commanded thee of God."*
ACTS 10:33

This voice out of the congregation is at once humbling and encouraging. Humbling—because who am I, who is any man, to interpret the mind of God? Encouraging—because it puts the emphasis so squarely on the really important thing. This is the House of God, and we have not turned into it as into a secular meeting place. It is God's presence we have come seeking, God's Word we need to hear. This narrative in Acts ought to have something cogent and compelling to say to us today.

You remember the story. It was one of the most dramatic moments in the history of the early church. It shows the gospel moving out from its original setting in Judea into the mainstream of history and the arena of the wider world.

Here was this Roman officer Cornelius, stationed in Palestine at Caesarea, a representative of the imperial power in occupied territory. He was a soldier of the finest type, beloved by his men, respected by all who knew him. Being a devout and openminded man, there in Caesarea he had come under the influence of the Jewish religion. He had come to know and to revere the God of Israel, the Lord of hosts. He had been deeply impressed by Judaism's code of ethics. He had learned to pray. Yet he was not content. He was a Roman, brought up in a pagan tradition. Perhaps Israel's God was not for him? Perhaps he would be a fool even to think of embracing a conquered people's faith? And yet, it seemed so much deeper and more spiritual than anything the gods of Rome had taught him. And there was that dream which had come to him one night—or was it an angel? Was it perhaps God himself giving him a sign that he should investigate further? He decided to act upon it. He would settle this one way or the other. He sent messengers to seek out someone to set his doubts at rest.

This is where the second main actor in the drama appears. It was Peter's habit to go up to the housetop for his daily quiet time of meditation and devotion. Peter, you must remember, was still very much a Jew at heart, a crypto-nationalist, with considerable mental reservations about the wisdom of a universal church or a Gentile mission. Then one day on the housetop he had a strange vision. It indicated that, now that Christ had come, the barriers were down; all men everywhere were brothers, and he must act accordingly. He was still deeply pondering the vision, when suddenly—shattering his reverie—there was a loud knock at the door beneath.

It was Cornelius's men, come to summon him. And Peter —his spirit still bathed in the afterglow of the housetop vision, still vibrant from communion with the high God of his salvation—rose and went with them. He went not knowing what to expect, but feeling in a strange way that it was not only a detachment of Roman soldiers who had arrived at his gate and rudely interrupted his vision: the disturbing voice, he vaguely felt, had been the voice of Christ himself, "Behold, I stand at the door and knock."

When he arrived at his destination, it was to find quite a considerable company awaiting him—Cornelius and his family and friends, with some members of the occupying garrison, and some Jews from the local synagogue. "Why have you sent for me?" asked Peter. And Cornelius told him of the dream— or was it an angel?—urging him to do just this. "You have done well to come," said Cornelius, "and I am grateful." And then followed the words of that momentous invitation, "Now therefore are we all here present before God, to hear all things that are commanded thee of God."

Now of course, in a sense, this dramatic incident stands

apart by itself. It was a historic and decisive turning point in the development of the apostolic mission. It was Christ breaking down another wall of partition. And yet, if you look at it again, does it not represent what happens, or at any rate what ideally ought to happen, whenever a congregation meets for worship? Let us look at it today in this light and see what it has to tell us.

There is, first, *the expectancy of the atmosphere.* The very narrative in Acts throbs with it. Cornelius had been praying about this gathering and what might come of it, and when you get that kind of prayer and expectation mingled, some kind of Pentecostal blessing is almost bound to happen. Peter could not possibly fail in his mission, with this spirit to help him. In fact, here in this Roman officer's house you have something of the same kind of expectancy that had stirred not long before in Galilean and Judean villages when word went round that the Prophet of Nazareth, Jesus the healer and teacher, was about to pass their way. The Gospels show you that: people streaming out from the narrow lanes, straining their eyes to the horizon, wondering, "Will he perhaps turn and look on me? Will he perhaps even speak to me? Shall I have a chance to tell him of my problem and find help and healing for my need?"

But that, you tell me, was long ago and far away, and nothing like it is to be looked for now. I wonder. Are you so sure? Listen to this. "Where two or three are gathered in my name," said Jesus, "there am I in the midst of them." It is the Master's word of honor. And it means that in any ordinary gathering for worship he is quite certain to be there. As if indeed any gathering could be ordinary after that! How could worship ever be ordinary, dull, lifeless, conventional if we really took that shining, infallible promise to our hearts? If a whole congregation came expectantly, would not the power of the Spirit be released to heal and bless and quicken and make new? It is here that the renewal of the church will begin—when quite simply and very expectantly we take Jesus at his word.

Observe, further, how Acts underlines, not only the expectancy of the atmosphere, but also *the unanimity of the congregation.* "We are *all here present* before God." No one who could have been there had stayed away. Important issues were pending, and no one was willing to be left out.

Do you remember, in the story of the first Easter, when the upper room grew luminous with the presence of the Lord, how one poignant note intrudes into the narrative? "Thomas was not present with them when Jesus came." So one disciple missed the sunrise. And so for another week he had to carry his unresolved doubt locked up in his lonely, brooding heart. "Do not forsake," appeals a New Testament apostle, "the assembling of yourselves together." When a congregation does assemble, its unanimity is not of course unanimity of opinion whether ecclesiastical or political, nor is it any stereotyping of individuality, similarity of social grouping, cultural background, or anything of the kind. The more diversity there the better. It is the unanimity, conscious or unconscious, of personal need, the pressure of the great elemental human questions: What does this life mean, when all is said and done, this life so transient and time so irreversible? What significance can my poor creaturely existence, with its threescore years and ten, have against the vast rolling aeons of the cosmos? Why is the pilgrim way beset by so many formidable obstacles, sore partings, and all the heartache and vicissitudes that flesh is heir to? That is why to anyone with some imagination a gathered congregation is such a moving sight. Who can tell what hopes and fears are present there, what yearning aspirations, crippling burdens, fierce temptations, inner lonelinesses, longings for the light? This, amid all diversity, is the uniting factor, binding all together. "We are all here present before God."

Notice, in the third place, that we have here *the awareness of the eternal.* "We are all here present *before God.*" Cornelius, in his own dim way, had begun to see that Rome and the emperor whom he served were not life's ultimate realities. He had sensed something mysterious, transcendent, as though a greater empire were claiming his allegiance. It is indeed this sense of mystery and transcendence which is the very life of the church's worship. Here is this tumultuous, absorbing, hectoring world of sense and time in which our lives are set. We need desperately to be reminded of the dimension of eternity. We need to experience a stretching of our horizons, the linking up of our human environment with something away beyond this world, the interpenetration of the natural by the supernatural. We need something to sharpen our awareness of Almighty God.

That awareness of God is your birthright. It was born into you when he created you in his own image, imprinted his likeness upon you, and breathed his spirit into your inmost being. It was sealed for you when he wrote his law upon your heart and made you restless till you rest in him. But unless it is trained and nurtured, the world can all too easily smother and destroy it. That is happening all the time. One thing the worship of the church should be doing is precisely to keep that God-awareness vivid and alive. A church that fails here— whatever else its honorable achievements—fails all along the line. Leave out from any worship gathering what is essentially supernatural, the depths of mystery and the heights of transcendence, and what is left? Certainly nothing to bow the heart in adoration or to convert the world. One thing is needful— and how it rebukes every casual attitude, every flippant world! "We are all here present before God."

A further fact relevant to the worship of the church now emerges from our text. This is *the challenge to the preacher.* "We are present, to hear *all things that are commanded thee of God.*" Cornelius was wanting from Peter—what? Certainly not any personal views and opinions—about the relative merits, for instance, of Roman law and Jewish. He had not summoned this man to his presence for a polite political dialogue or a comfortable philosophical debate. It was answers he wanted, not problems; certainties, not speculations; a divine authenticated word, not theories and impressions.

This is the challenge to the preacher still—"all things that are commanded thee by God." It is the same challenge with which, long before Cornelius and Peter, a king in Judah had approached the prophet Jeremiah: "Tell me, is there any word from the Lord?" Apparently King Zedekiah had grown somewhat tired of listening to the voices of the hour, Egypt, Assyria, and all the rest of them, the conflicting words that kept issuing from one seat of government after another, or from this sect of astrologers, that group of theological innovators, and so forth—just as we today can grow tired of the bombarding incessant words from rival camps. "Now," said he, "give me a word from the Lord!"

This is the challenge to the preacher. I know that this raises the whole question of authority, which is so much at issue today. I know that the mood of the hour might seem to favor an utterance deferential and apologetic, full of qualifications and liberally studded with interrogation marks. And indeed there is a dogmatism that would ill befit anyone who has felt in his own soul some touch of the majesty and the mystery whose judgments are unsearchable and whose ways past finding out. But just because such a specious authoritarianism can exist, is that any reason why the trumpet should give an uncertain sound? After all, what is it that we are hoping may come through to us in a church service? Not surely any man's notions about God, but God himself in omnipotent action, God giving himself to us at the point of our most intimate need.

What Cornelius was wanting from Peter was not guesswork, hearsay, theological puzzles; it was "Thus saith the Lord!" Not argument, but news. Not stones, but bread. And he had a right to ask it, as Peter had a right to give it. If God has said to me (as he has done again and again), "My grace is sufficient for thee," and if he has verified it in experience, I should be an ungrateful fool or a knave to make no sign and to leave the field open to those who are busy telling this generation that God does not even exist. In the words of a New Testament apostle, "What our eyes have seen of the Word of life, our ears have heard, our hands have handled, this declare we unto you!"

So here is the story Cornelius's request elicited Peter's response. The challenge to the preacher leads on to *the outcome of the proclamation.* It was indeed news that Peter brought, news much more wonderful and momentous than anything Caesarea had ever heard, news of the breakthrough into human life of a power more world-shattering and renewing by far than anything imperial Rome could boast. It is only an epitome of that historic sermon that the author of Acts can give, but read it, and see if it is not the whole gospel in miniature. Straight to the heart of divine revelation it goes—to incarnate God in Bethlehem and Galilee, God in Jesus of Nazareth healing the sick, delivering the captives, forgiving the sinful, on beyond that to the passion, the cross, the resurrection, the defeat of the powers of darkness, the opening of the kingdom to all believers. It was at that point that something happened to the congregation. Acts says the Holy Spirit fell upon them. It was God through the Holy Ghost revealing to them the reality of his mighty act in Christ and flooding them with fullness of life.

Will a day come when what happened there to Cornelius and his friends breaks in again upon the church and the world with sudden life-giving renewal? It is not impossible—if the church's worship is Christ-centered, with the realization that in seeing Jesus we are gazing into the very eyes of eternal God. But whether that great worldwide revival of which some of us dream and for which we pray should be just round the next corner of the road or far away down distant years, one thing is certain: in less dramatic and more secret ways something like it can be happening all the time—the breath of God breathing upon one soul here and another there, the quiet stirring of God's Spirit in my heart, to send me back to life with new resolve and a surer grasp of Christ's dear strengthening hand. This can and does happen. Every day it is happening somewhere. I pray it may be happening here now.

> Spirit of purity and grace,
> Our weakness, pitying, see.

Take that familiar prayer today, and if you feel it is not quite personal enough, then in the silence now make it even more intimately your own:

> Spirit of purity and grace,
> My weakness, pitying, see;
> O make my heart Thy dwelling-place,
> And worthier Thee.

We have been "all here present before God" today. And so now, from this service, we go back to our several tasks and to the daily pilgrimage with a new meaning and purpose in life, a new song ringing and singing in our hearts, and the whole world full of God's glory.

THE PRESSURE OF LIFE
AND THE PEACE OF GOD

*"O Lord our God, we rest on Thee,
and in Thy name we go against this multitude."*
2 CHRONICLES 14:11

Here you have a picture of the night before a battle. Here were Asa king of Judah and his valiant army caught and cornered, with enemy battalions to right and left of them and all around them, no earthly chance of extricating themselves from the trap, no hope of mercy if they asked a truce, no expedient left but to fling themselves on that terrible armored circle round them and sell their lives as dearly as they could. And the hours of night dragged past so slowly, and there was sleep for none around the watchfires in the camp; and men were peering away to the East wishing the dawn would come and this awful suspense be over; others were thinking of the homes they had said good-bye to perhaps for ever, remembering how someone with tears in her eyes had stood at the cottage door back among the Judean hills, and the children had clung to their father's neck and kissed him, crying "Come back soon" as he went down the road, "Come back safe and soon!" It all seemed so long ago. Then suddenly the silence was broken by a ringing shout, "Watchman, what of the night?" and the watchman cried, "The morning comes," and men looked and the East was growing gray, and they started buckling on their armor. Some were laughing and jesting, as men have always jested face to face with death; some were tense and silent, and some were wondering, "Where is our leader and commander? Why is he not here to rally us? Where is the king?" Yonder alone by himself in his tent the king was on his knees. "Asa," says the

chronicler, "cried unto the Lord his God." He had been praying half the night, wrestling in prayer. Had God cast his people
off? Had he left them to their fate? "Lord God, art thou
asleep? Must I cry louder to wake thee?" But in the dawning
a strange thing happened. A wonderful peace came stealing
into Asa's heart: after the night of stormy doubt and wrestling,
a divine mysterious tranquillity. "O Lord our God," and his
voice was calm and steady now, "we rest on thee, and in thy
name we go against this multitude." Then he rose, went out, and
gave the signal for the attack.

Now just to read this old story in the Book of Chronicles is
surely to realize in a flash its relevance for today. How apposite
to our contemporary situation! "Against this multitude," what
a daunting multitude of problems—economic, industrial, social,
international, moral—we have to go out against today! Or take
it on the more personal level. "This multitude," the whole
menacing multitude of anxieties and complications that life deals
out to us today, the scramble of business, the strain of competition, the burden and the heat, the wear and tear, the insecurity
of being young, the loneliness of growing old, all the thousand
anxieties that paralyze our faith and corrupt our consecration—
against all that, in thy name, O God! I almost feel that instead
of trying to preach on this text it would be better just to repeat
it over and again. I hope at any rate there will be some who
will do that, today and tomorrow and through the days ahead.
For I am sure that, if it sinks right in, it can come upon us as
an authentic voice from heaven, enabling us to lift up our heads
and face life without weakness or dishonor. "O God, we rest
on thee, and in thy name we go against this multitude."

Take this part of the prayer first: "O God, we rest on Thee."
Asa could say that. Most of us cannot. Would we not have to
confess it is precisely such restfulness and poise of spirit that
we so badly lack? When Jesus said, "Learn of me, and ye shall
find rest to your souls," it was a lesson which even some most
devoted, active Christians are terribly slow to learn.

"Things," said Emerson bitterly, "are in the saddle and ride mankind." How much truer that is today than when Emerson wrote the words! It is true of our modern civilization. An affluent society has wonderful assets in which as Christians we can ungrudgingly rejoice. But it has frightening liabilities too. One of the most ominous is the overactivism induced by the endless possibilities now within grasp, the obsession with trivialities, the inability to relax. For the technology that multiplies our resources and the automation that increases our leisure have not begun to answer the questions "What are we here for? Where have we come from, and where are we going, and what is the ultimate purpose of it all?" and therefore they cannot give us an undistracted mind and a heart at rest. There is a horrible despotism today of things and gadgets, the tension of being always on the go, an anxiety complex of not being in with the crowd, and absence of the spirit of inwardness, a dread of being alone.

Even the church is infected by this prevalent mood. We feel that there is not enough happening in the church. That is probably perfectly true. The church's impact on society is only fractional compared with what it ought to be. But when we want to do something about it, so often our first impulse is to say, "We must get busy and overhaul the organization, we must oil the ecclesiastical machinery, we must demand that our divinity colleges turn out skilled administrators above everything else, we must institute a new kind of propaganda, set up another committee, resuscitate the parochial system, democratize our structures." God forgive us! That is what we concentrate on. And no doubt, in a way, it is important enough. But are there no prior questions? Have we been giving the Holy Spirit room to work? Are we waiting on the Lord to renew our strength? Are we alive to the reality of the supernatural? Do we know what it means to say "O Lord our God, we rest on thee"?

What of ourselves? "I don't know how I'll ever get through this next year," one finds himself saying. Or, "This drive of competition is wearing me out and getting me down." Or, "My children—what will they make of it when they have to go out into this dangerous world with its delusive promises and subtle temptations and uninhibited permissiveness?" Or, "If I had a different psychological outfit, a stronger physique, a less exacting job, I could stop worrying. But as it is, how can I help it?" Yes, Emerson was right, "Things are in the saddle and ride mankind."

Even the saints have confessed it. There was one of the noblest of the psalmists who was experiencing this very thing—pushed by the pressure of life to the verge of nervous collapse. "O that I had wings," he cried, "wings like a dove, for then would I fly away and be at rest." Mendelssohn's haunting setting of the words to one of his loveliest melodies can almost bring the tears to one's eyes, "O for the wings, for the wings of a dove, Far away, far away would I rove."

But this is the Lord's Day and the Lord's House, and our very presence here today means "Surely there must be a better way!" And indeed there is—as even the psalmist came to see. You do not need any alien wings or any far wilderness to fly to; you do not need any mystical sentimental escape from the battering siege of stern realities. You can stand surrounded—like Asa king of Judah—by whole battalions of harsh-featured facts and find your peace, your victory, not somewhere else on borrowed wings, but right there, precisely there—if (and this is the point) you have learned from the heart to say, "O Lord my God, I rest on thee!"

There are multitudes of people today, many of them making no religious professions whatever, who would give almost anything to escape from the sense of meaninglessness and anxiety and boredom and find the secret of a confident serenity. I remember reading an article by that excellent novelist and literary critic Ernest Raymond, in which he was reviewing a book of sermons; he described the most impressive sermon he himself had ever listened to in all his life. Intellectually, he said, this particular sermon was negligible; in its text and texture it was utterly trite; its delivery was abominable. And yet, there was a something. It was during the war, and a group of men had gathered in a cellar to hear a sermon by an Anglo-Catholic father, expecting perhaps some dry-as-dust theology or some bombastic oratory about the God of battles and the rightness of their cause. But instead of that, the preacher, sitting down and staring at the floor or ceiling in search of words, so halting was his speech, spoke of the text, "Come unto me, all ye who labor and are heavy-laden, and I will give you rest." "I think he spoke for an hour," said Raymond, "and not a man of us moved, and most of us were very quiet all that night thereafter." Does that not go right to the heart of things? Is not that what most of us are craving more than we can tell—something to hold us poised and calm and restful,

> Though hills amidst the seas be cast,
> Though waters roaring make,

something to stabilize our staggering souls? "O God, thou hast made us for thyself, and our heart is restless until it rest in thee."

One there was who knew it utterly. Look at the life of Jesus, battered and besieged by man's despising and rejecting—what pressures toward breakdown and collapse were there, what frustrations and thwartings, misunderstandings and hatreds! Across the centuries comes the shouting of a multitude, loud, violent, terrible: "This is not Messiah! This man is a menace to our ambitions. Away with him, crucify him!" And through it all—this is the amazing, incredible thing—the deep hush of a conquering peace and an ineffable serenity. Was not this the inner secret of Nazareth and Jerusalem and Olivet and Calvary, "Father, into thy hands I commend my spirit; O Lord my God, I rest on thee"?

"Yes," someone may say, "but that was Jesus. How am I to set about it? What am I to do? Is there any practical action I can take?" The Word of God says there is. It prescribes three basic facts to fix on. It promises that if you do concentrate your mind on these, first thing in the morning and last thing at night, you will not be dragged helpless at the heels of circumstance. You will be more than conqueror.

Fact number one—*the sovereignty of God*. The Bible says, Build on that rock. The Lord God omnipotent reigneth. You confess it every time you say your creed, "I believe in God the Father Almighty." You acknowledge it every time you repeat the Lord's Prayer, "Thine is the kingdom, the power and the glory." Well then, believe your own faith! The trouble is that we may believe it theoretically without ever seeing it, imagining it, realizing it in its exciting dramatic reality. Coventry Patmore has told how once, as a boy of eleven, he was reading a book, when all of a sudden (he says), "it struck me what an exceedingly fine thing it would be if there really was a God." That is what some of us are needing still—something more than a vague acceptance of doctrines and beliefs—to be struck, struck all of a heap, if you like, by the sudden, shattering realization that these things which our conventional, facile words repeat are shiningly and exhilaratingly true. God lives. God reigns. God has engraved his own image indelibly on every man alive, so that I cannot meet my neighbor without meeting something of God. God has all the world—its atomic science, its space technology, its politics, its hopes and dreams and terrible dreads—in the hollow of his hand. God, with all the universe to govern, has nevertheless come down the road of my life, seeking me. From hour to hour, he is my Father. From everlasting to everlasting, he is God. Great peace have they who rest their minds on that.

The sovereignty of God. Fact number two: *the presence of Christ*. "Lo, I am with you always, to the very end of the world." The One who spoke these words is present with us at this moment. This is no romantic mysticism or pious rhetoric, but solid, essential fact. "I am with you always." It is certain, quite certain, that he is here. "Where two or three are gathered in my name, there am I in the midst of them." He said it. And he meant it. Today from your deep inmost heart, with awe and gladness, you can say, "Yes, Jesus, Master, it is true! It is really true. You have kept your promise. You are here! You are with me now. You are always with me. My physical eyes cannot see you, for the veil of sense impedes, but I know that, as truly as you were in Galilee, so certain is it that you are with us now, making the darkness of our poor human fumbling and faltering luminous with your presence, able to save and heal us all!" There was an old peasant in a French village, who for an hour before going into the fields in the early morning visited the little church, and for an hour at the close of his labor resumed his vigil, and when his priest asked him what he did in those hours so punctually spent, he replied, "I just look at Christ, and he looks at me." He gave two hours to it. If only we would give ten minutes, it might transform life out of recognition. Or take the other end of the ecumenical line. Here is Catherine Booth of the Salvation Army. At first she was reluctant to accompany her husband on the great adventure of faith, but facing her decision, she said, she encountered Christ. "He did not smile at me, nor did he chide, but raised his hand, and I saw the nailprints on it. 'That is your way,' he said, 'and there is no other.' And I said, 'So be it, Lord. Will you go with me?' 'I will be with you,' he answered, 'to the end.'" The living Presence! "The Lord Jesus," said Paul, of a dreadfully difficult and discouraging period of his life, "stood at my side and put strength into me." And the same Christ who was with Paul on that difficult road, with Samuel Rutherford and John Bunyan in captivity, with David Livingstone in darkest Africa, with Dietrich Bonhöffer in Hitler's prison, with a minister friend of my own who died far too young, as we might think, and who ten days before he died, and knowing that he was dying, wrote to me a wonderful letter full of the loving kindness and tender mercy of the Lord—that same Christ looks into your eyes and mine, saying "Lo, as I was with all of these, so am I today with you." "As with them, so with you." What peace to know that when you need help most, he is quite certain to be there!

The sovereignty of God, the presence of Christ, and finally, fact number three: *the power of the Spirit.* This is a doctrine our earthbound minds are terribly slow to believe; we have neglected it, to our sore impoverishment. If we really believed it—that the power of God is available to flood the church, to heal the nations, to cast out our own particular private devil here and now—if we really believed this, you would not have the shameful spectacle of Christians being as downhearted and defeatist as any believer. But as things are, if the power of the Spirit were suddenly to break in on the international scene and check the Gadarene insanity of nuclear devilry; if the power of the Spirit were suddenly to thaw out the refrigerating conventions of formal worship; if the power of the Spirit were suddenly this very day to visit our life, piercing the gloom of apathy and half belief, and making our feeble aspirations radiant and triumphant—if that were to happen, we should doubtless be astonished and surprised. What right have we to be astonished and surprised? For all that is promised on the word of God himself. Why should we live as though the word of God were a myth, as though Jesus had never happened, as though there were something strange in the promises coming true?

I am not condemning anyone, God forbid. I am accusing myself. "Lord, I believe; help thou my unbelief." For this thing is true. It is not belief that is credulous. It is unbelief that is so illogical and callow and absurd. Either there is no spiritual meaning in the universe, and when Jesus said, "If you give good gifts to your children how much more will your heavenly Father give the Holy Spirit to them who ask him," it was just talk and illusion and hallucination—in which case every church might as well be shut down today and never opened again; either that, or else we really do have a gospel that dries all tears and lifts all burdens and snaps all chains; we really are in touch with a Power compared with which all the pomps and material circumstance of earth are puny and pathetic and ridiculous. "Lord, I believe." I know this thing is true. I know the power of the Spirit can refashion the chaos of the world, rejuvenate the church, and flood every frightened, faltering soul with freedom, joy, and peace.

There, then, are our three facts—the sovereignty of God, the presence of Christ, the power of the Spirit. What we have to do is to fix our mind on them deliberately, consciously, making time for this every day by prayer, meditation, recollection. The best result of this service today would be that someone here should resolve upon a more disciplined devotional life, making some time every day to realize all over again the divine transcendent resources which make all things possible and the everlasting mercy by which all sins are forgiven. It can be such a transforming thing to be able to say to life's thronging, distracting cares "Stand back, O world, and let me stay my mind on God!" "Thou wilt keep him in perfect peace, whose mind is stayed on thee."

Remember, in closing, what Asa added. "O Lord our God, we rest on thee; *and in thy name we go against this multitude.*" Look at this last glimpse of Asa king of Judah. He is off his knees now. He is out of his tent. He is at the head of his army. He is leading the attack. And now the legions of the enemy are wavering, their armor-clad battalions breaking, scattering to the four winds.

What is religion? Not just resting on God (which might be a selfish monasticism), but resting on God and then riding out to encounter all the problems, difficulties, temptations the day may bring. Not just keeping vigil at the altar, but rising when the vigil is over, with the trumpet sounding for a new crusade. "O Lord our God, we rest on thee, and in thy name we go against this multitude."

The old Greek Archimedes used to say that, if he were given three things, it would be possible, physically, scientifically possible to move the earth off its axis. "Give me a standing place out yonder in space, a fulcrum, and a lever long enough and strong enough, and I will move the world!" We Christians have our standing place, the Rock of Ages, the sovereignty of God. We have our fulcrum, the friendship and the fellowship of Christ. We have our lever, the power of the Spirit. Why should we not move the world? Given these, all things are possible. We can master life and conquer death and storm the battlements of heaven.

This is the victory. And it is for you.

THE VICTORY OF FAITH

"Lord, how are they increased that trouble me!
Many are they that rise up against me. Many there be which say of my soul,
There is no help for him in God. But Thou, O Lord, art a shield for me;
my glory and the lifter up of mine head.
I cried unto the Lord with my voice,
and He heard me out of His holy hill. I laid me down and slept;
I awaked: for the Lord sustained me.
I will not be afraid of ten thousands of people,
that have set themselves against me round about. Arise, O Lord; save me,
O my God; for Thou hast smitten all mine enemies upon the cheek bone;
Thou hast broken the teeth of the ungodly.
Salvation belongeth unto the Lord; Thy blessing is upon Thy people."

PSALM 3

It is a moving thought that the psalms we sing in church or read at home were all well known to Jesus. He sang them with his disciples, pondered over them and quoted them, found his own experience mirrored in them. So when we meditate on the Psalms today, we are drawing on the same wellspring at which our Lord refreshed his soul. Should we not turn to them far more frequently and expectantly, remembering what they meant to the dear Savior of us all? Who so likely as he to help us appropriate their treasure? What voice so sure as his to interpret for us their meaning?

Take this Third Psalm. If ever you have tried to grapple seriously with the grim anomalies and perplexities of life; if ever such endemic facts as war and violence, natural calamity, and man's inhumanity to man have seemed to you to make savage mockery of human dreams; if ever, being young, you have found life being less than kindly to your hopes; or if ever, being old, it has failed to provide the relief and relaxation you expected from advancing years, and instead has left you struggling with sorely diminished resilience to cope with its demands; in short, if trouble—whether it be personal trouble or the harsh reality of the confusion and chaos of the world—if trouble has bombarded your mind with questioning and your soul with doubt, then this psalm is for you. For the psalmist himself has been there.

There are good grounds for accepting the tradition that this is indeed a psalm of David, belonging to the time when rebel factions had dethroned him and driven him from Zion, an outlaw without a home. Read it again with that background in mind, and how vivid it all becomes! And how piercingly the greater Son of David must have seen his destiny prefigured.

When we bring it to the standpoint of our own experience, what facets of truth do we find illuminated? There is a whole series of them, and I ask you to notice just a few.

First, this: *the inherent mystery of life.* Why should the divine providence that had called David from the sheepfold to the throne not have kept him there secure? Why should the greater Son of David, coming to his own world in the fullness of the time, have had nowhere to lay his head? Why should the long centuries of history have such deplorable tales to tell of strife begetting strife—with no end even today, when destruction waxes ever more destructive and barbarism more barbaric? And on the more personal level, why should life deal out to us so many unforeseen problems, so much that puts our happiness at risk and runs right counter to our plans? And in any case, what is the sense of an existence doomed to be negated sooner or later by the inexorability of death?

If ever you find this burden of the mystery of life weighing upon you, there are two things to remember.

One is that you are in good company. It is not your solitary problem. Emphatically not. All the saints have grappled with it. More than any other, Jesus faced and fought it. He wrestled with it until, as the evangelist says, his sweat was like blood. Will the thought of that high company not brace your spirit?

The other thing to remember is suggested by our psalm. For this man's first word is "Lord." "O Lord, how are they increased that trouble me!" In other words, when you are up against it, get back to God. This man will not mention his trouble to anyone, nor even to his own soul, until he has set down the divine name first. That is the proper strategy. Link your finite resources with eternity. Get back to God! The one place to join issue with the mystery of life is in the light of God's countenance.

But now this brings us to the second fact the psalm exemplifies. This is *the strange silence of God.* "Many there be who say of my soul, 'There is no help for him in God.' " That is the devil's taunt. That was precisely how Satan tempted Christ. "Come down from the cross, Christ, King of Israel, that we may see and believe!" "He trusted in God that he would deliver him: let him deliver him now, if he delight in him!" That is the devil, and David knew it, and Jesus knew it. But there was this difference—that David in the hour of his calamity almost began to wonder whether it might not be true. That was the worst of his plight, far worse than the loss of his throne and the vagabond life that followed it—the thought that perhaps God had temporarily or finally deserted him. "Lead, kindly light, amid the encircling gloom." Yes, that may be all very well, but what if the kindly light itself one day begins to flicker and go out? What if God should disappoint and divine providence leave you in the lurch? What if the whole thing is fantasy, irrelevant, inconsequential? "There is no help for him in God," mocked David's enemies. Poor wretch, thinking he could fall back upon some inner shrine, some inviolable fortress, and then—when he did fall back upon it—finding that central citadel wrecked and desolate! No help in God. No way nor truth nor life in Christ. Then indeed "chaos is come again."

It is the devil's voice. But see how it leads on immediately to the third fact the psalm incorporates. This is *the defiant reaffirming of faith.* "But thou, Lord, art a shield for me, my glory, and the lifter up of my head." Is that not magnificent? Notice, it is not "Lord, please be a shield." It is not "Oh that the Lord would see the fiery darts of my foes, and provide me with a shield!" "Thou *art* a shield." That is faith as affirmation, flung in the face of the devil's subtlety. We are needing today far more of this robust and positive brand of faith, not a continual anxious balancing of possibilities, not a vague hope that, if only we can hang on long enough, somehow, somewhere, something will transpire to see us through our predicament, but this note of plain, straight, categorical affirmation, "Thou art my shield and my glory!"

And note the lovely expression that follows, "Thou art the lifter up of my head." To grasp the real significance of this, you have to remember that David—unlike the greater Son of David who was to come—was a stumbling sinful creature, and bitterly he knew it. Never to his dying day would he forget the terrible hour when God had had to send Nathan the prophet to rebuke him with the rapier-thrust "Thou art the man!" Indeed the real sting of his present plight as exile and alien was precisely that he himself was largely to blame for it: a realization to bow his heart in despondency and his head in shame. But listen to this, when for you or for me the sense of unworthiness becomes acute, "Thou art the lifter up of my head." So it was when the Risen Christ sought out the disciple who had shamefully disowned him, and recommissioned him to be an apostle, saying to him "Feed my lambs." And Peter tried almost incredulously to realize it: "He means me, who flouted and disclaimed him. Can it be? It can't. And yet—I wonder? Yes, it must! If he says it, it is true. Nothing else matters. The nightmare is over. The devil of doubt is impotent. And if the Lord can trust me so, I can look the whole world in the face. Thou art the lifter up of my head!" David in the Old Testament, and Peter in the New, are just ourselves. That is why the old Bible is so modern and contemporary. It requires no tricks or manipulation to bring it up-to-date. It is our story. You are in this psalm. And so am I. And because of that, if you can believe it, there is no low mood you cannot smite hip and thigh. Let the devil of depression practice all his wiles— in Christ, you have taken his measure. You can spurn him back to the hell where he belongs. "Lord, thou art the lifter up of my head." This is the defiant reaffirming of faith. All the promises of Christ belong to you.

Midst flaming worlds, in these arrayed,
With joy shall I lift up my head.

Now, following the psalm further, we come to this: *the
miraculous power of prayer.* "I cried to the Lord with my voice,
and he heard me out of his holy hill." Note these past tenses.
They mean that the psalmist is working from a basis of actual
proved experience. He is bringing in memory to reinforce hope.
He is saying to us in effect, "I could tell you how once and again,
here and there and yonder, my prayers were answered. There
stands the evidence. Believe? Why should I not believe? Is it so
irrational to accept the force of the evidence?" Today in this confused, bewildered world this is still the irrefragable argument for
faith. And if there is one thing far more impressive than all the
massive arguments of philosophers and all the debates of schools
of theology ancient and modern, it is the fact of men and women
of holy and humble heart saying quite simply, "I have the evidence. I cried to the Lord; he heard and answered me." The
strength of the church is that you will find such folk in any Christian congregation, anywhere. "The heaven of heavens cannot
contain thee," cries Thomas à Kempis in breathless amazement,
"and yet thou sayest, Come ye all to me!" Here is a Bible miracle
that is continually being reproduced in humble lives.

I make no apology for using the word "miracle." If answers
to prayer are not miracle, nothing is. For who is it to whom our
prayers are addressed? Not to our subconscious mind. It is God
the transcendent, God who counts the stars, God by whose will
all the immeasurable universes exist, and on whose will every
beat of our hearts depends, so that if the active will were for
one moment to be withdrawn the whole creation and every one
of us here would immediately disintegrate and cease to be. Do
not be misled by the stultifying theological trends that would
desupernaturalize the transcendent. God is transcendent purpose,
sovereign freedom, the cosmic mind, the loving personal will
that holds our mortal lives in being. It is to him our prayers
ascend, through Christ our mediator and intercessor. "I cried
unto the Lord, and he heard me out of his holy hill."

There follows, as an immediate and inevitable result, another aspect of the psalmist's discovery: *the precious gift of serenity.* "I lay down and slept; I awaked, for the Lord sustained me." He is away beyond his worrying now, for is not God alive and wakeful all the time? Not that the rough winds of trouble had ceased to blow for David; there were still grim foes surrounding him and desperate hazards to be endured. And no man in this world is offered a cheap immunity. That is why one has to be specially careful in talking about this matter of inner peace and serenity. There is a way of reproving folk for their anxieties which—even when it is done in the name of religion—is irritating, indeed cruel and heartless: as though the possession of a calm mind were simply a matter of mental psychology or spiritual gymnastics and could be cultivated by the practice of some obvious techniques.

But all that pious talk is a caricature of Bible truth. It is a far cry from what Paul was describing when, awaiting Nero's judgment in a Roman prison, he wrote about "the peace of God standing armed and sentinel over heart and mind." It is nowhere in sight of what Jesus was doing when, with the cross and the final dereliction looming over him, he was able to make the upper room of the Last Supper luminous with a radiant serenity, "My peace I give to you." You need the God of David and of Paul and of Jesus Christ for that. You need the God whose love moves the stars and permeates the universe and undergirds your life and sees the end from the beginning. You need the God by the indwelling of whose Spirit in receptive hearts every conceivable circumstance of our mortal life can be irradiated and transcended and transfigured. It is this dimension of eternity, this basic and essential relationship to a Father Almighty, unslumbering and unsleeping, that gives the perspective from which alone the precious gift of serenity can come. "I lay down and slept; I awaked, for the Lord sustained me."

And now the final facet of truth this psalm illumines: *the measureless scope of salvation.* "Salvation belongs unto the Lord: thy blessing be upon thy people." "Thy people," that meant for David his nation, the whole Israelite community, including therefore the rebels who had outlawed and dethroned him. "Thy blessing upon them!" This is David, in the magnanimity of his heart, anticipating his greater Son who was to intercede even for those who were cursing him and driving in the nails, "Father, forgive them!" For "salvation," the saving power of God, is not to be defeated in its purpose. It triumphs over hostility and adversity and all the demonism of history and includes the whole creation in its measureless embrace.

Indeed, the faith which Christ has taught declares that it goes even further than this, that the saving passion of God embraces in its scope not only this present life, but a life beyond. If you know something of what it means to call God "Father," as Jesus taught us all to do; if God has sealed something of his image upon you and put some portion of his Spirit into you, thus for ever differentiating your human nature from all other created things and kindling within you aspirations which no earthly joys can finally satisfy; if from time to time the stirring of God's Spirit within you reminds you that you are a pilgrim and a stranger on the earth—then you may be utterly sure that the divine Hand which created you at the first can recreate you and will recreate you at the last.

This is the measureless, exhilarating scope of the gospel you and I have received from Christ. It embraces not only today and tomorrow and next year and all the "threescore years and ten," but reaches out also into the far vistas of eternity and the glories of the New Jerusalem. Surely, given a faith of such dimensions, we have no right to be dull, conventionalized, lackluster Christians. We ought to be rejoicing and exulting in it—yes, even when the road grows rough beneath our feet and perplexities thicken around our path—triumphing in it as we fare onward on our way, reinforced by its splendor and guided by its marvellous light. And to the blessed God who has created us for this high destiny, to the dear Christ who has called us to be joint heirs with himself, and to the Holy Spirit who kindles immortal longings in our hearts, be praise, thanksgiving and glory now and for ever.

THE CHRIST
OF THE EMMAUS ROAD

"We trusted that it had been He which should have redeemed Israel."
LUKE 24:21

"We trusted it would have been he who should have redeemed Israel." We hoped in Christ, and it has come to nothing, for he is dead. That is the most crushing of disappointments. If even Christ is not to be relied on, where on earth are we to turn? If his teaching is illusory and his power a myth and his kingdom the insubstantial pageant of a dream, then indeed the fatalist is right: the world is bankrupt of hope, and chaos is come again. There are hundreds of disappointments in this life—we all have our share of them, and we have all caused some bad disappointments to others—but it is a dreadful heartbreaking hour when Jesus disappoints. We trusted he would have been the One to put our wrong world right.

This is quite certainly the root of a great amount of sincerely bewildered agnosticism today.

Here were these two men on the first Easter evening trudging dejectedly the seven-mile road from Jerusalem to Emmaus. Only a few days had elapsed since they had joined the throngs of pilgrims going up to the capital for the festival. And Cleopas and his friend had been so eager then and buoyant and excited. For might not this turn out to be the greatest festival of all? Jesus, so it was rumored, would be there. And who could tell but that this time he would assert himself and take political action and liberate their people from the tyrant's heel? What a day for Israel! "Arise, shine; for thy light is come, and the glory of the Lord is risen upon thee."

A few days ago! And now—this horrible disaster, this total

wreck of hope, this fierce, grim, hurting disillusionment. They had seen the procession of death coming out to Calvary. They had seen the crown of thorns, the jeering, hooting rabble, the squalor and ignominy and defeat. They had seen the poor broken body being taken down, when it was all over, to be hid away in the tomb. It was on this one Man, this Jesus, that all their hopes had centered. He was to sweep the world clean of social squalor and confusion and to bring in a millennium of peace and justice and prosperity. Well, it was all over; it would never happen now. Dead on a gallows, that lovely foolish dream they had cherished, crucified, dead, and buried once and for all.

Of all disappointments this is the most shattering. To be disappointed in Christ. To feel that perhaps God himself cannot be counted on to take a grip of the human situation. To find the beckoning dream of a better world and a Christianized society negated by new nightmares of nihilism and violence and inhumanity. To see the kingdom of heaven sabotaged by the strategies of Satan. It is not only the fool who says in his heart, There is no God. It is not only some self-conscious sophisticated latter-day theologians who have invented a "death of God" theology. Many an honestly bewildered soul today is facing that final doubt. For why, after nineteen centuries of Christ, is the world such a sorry shambles still? Why are the evil spirits and the powers of darkness so atrociously successful? "O God," cried a great warrior-prophet of long ago in an agony of disenchantment, "thou hast deceived me, and I have been deceived." That was Jeremiah, the day he felt like going on strike against such an impossible commission. Perhaps it is yourself. For it is not only the world's grim problems that are the trouble. There are such personal questions. Once perhaps you were told that religion would help you to build a character brave and strong and splendid and consistent. But it has not exactly worked out like that, has it? Perhaps you are still having to fight something you fought a dozen years ago. Or perhaps you are not fighting it now, for it has got you down, and you are feeling beaten, and the hope of the world is a lie. Perhaps we are all out on that Emmaus road today. Perhaps if our deepest inmost thoughts took words they would tell—like those two travelers—of scars of memory and broken hopes. "They have taken away my Lord, and I know not where they have laid him."

Comes faint and far Thy voice
From vales of Galilee,
Thy vision fades in ancient shades;
How should we follow Thee?

But wait! We are not alone upon that road. Suddenly the two wayfarers were joined by a third. He noticed that something was wrong. He rallied them on their doleful looks. "Why so sad?" And they gazed at him, astonished. "Have you not heard?" they asked. "But if you have come from Jerusalem, you must have heard. You have surely heard of the Prophet, the Nazarene, the Man who was to lead our nation and lift us from the dust. Do you mean to say that no one has told you what happened there two days ago to him? Did no one tell you of Calvary?" Imagine asking that Stranger that question, of all questions in the world! "Did no one tell you of Calvary?" "Their eyes," writes Luke, "were held fast, so that they should not know him."

And so often we are as blind as they. So often God in Christ is right there in front of us, in history and in the events of our own lives, and we do not recognize him. Not at the time. Afterwards, perhaps, like Jacob waking from his dream at Bethel: "Surely the Lord is in this place, and I knew it not." In retrospect today can you not see many points in your life when God must indeed have been there beside you, guiding, guarding, and defending, though you had no clear awareness of it at the time? There is a very moving confession in one of Joseph Addison's hymns:

When in the slippery paths of youth
With heedless steps I ran,
Thine arm, unseen, conveyed me safe,
And led me up to man.

We know what that means—slippery paths and many a precipice: and if you are still on the high road today or at least in sight of it, limping perhaps after a fall or two but still plodding on, don't thank your own wisdom for bringing you through. Don't thank your lucky stars. Thank the dear Savior of your soul. It is he who has been traveling there beside you, unrecognized. It is the rescuing energy of the eternal Christ.

Across a wide gulf of years there comes to me from student days the memory of a prayer that sealed this on my consciousness. It was the custom that a member of staff took college prayers on Mondays, while students conducted them on the other days of the week. There was a Monday morning when that great Old Testament scholar Professor Adam Welch—in many ways rather like a Hebrew prophet himself—startled us with his opening words. I suppose he had been becoming restive listening to so many student prayers beginning with the stereotyped phrase "O God, we come into thy presence." At any rate, this day the prayer began, "O God, we do *not* come into thy presence"; then a lengthened pause, and then, "for we are never anywhere else." I do not know if Dr. Welch was entirely right to use the act of prayer to administer the oblique rebuke. But certainly the essential truth of it was lodged that day in one student's mind at least. "We are never anywhere else." And this is the fact about the Risen Christ. He is here in this church. He is there at your own fireside. He will be there with you on the common road tomorrow. You are never left to face alone the untraveled way. Whether we recognize his presence or not, he is always there.

> Not where the wheeling systems darken,
> And our benumbed conceiving soars!—
> The drift of pinions, would we hearken,
> Beats at our own clay-shuttered doors.

Why do I believe in the resurrection? On the grounds of scriptural evidence—yes, indeed. But also because of direct encounter: God speaking to me in Christ in terms of personal experience in the here and now. It is because this can and does happen that belief in the resurrection does not mean a defying of reason; on the contrary, it means seeing the whole of life in the light of a new coherent rationality. Here it is the eternal that makes sense of the temporal. It is the supernatural that makes sense of an otherwise meaningless natural existence. This is the congruity of the resurrection with the facts of experience. This is the logic of faith.

But to return to the two men on the road. They did not recognize their Companion. But something was beginning to happen to them—something mysterious and significant, like a waft of the supernatural and the dawn of faith. "Did not our heart burn within us," they said afterwards, "as he talked with us on the way?" In the present climate of religious thought, this is something we ought to ponder. I beg you never to disparage or despise that burning heart which tells of Christ. We do manage, do we not, to take the gospel remarkably coolly and sedately, not to say casually? Occasionally I have had the experience of preaching in a church so sedate and cold and respectably formal that one almost wished its sedateness would be punctured by one uninhibited, resounding "Hallelujah!" There is a fine old Scottish paraphrase which, describing the work of the Holy Spirit in the church, has these lines:

> That heavenly Teacher, sent from God,
> Shall your whole soul inspire;
> Your minds shall fill with sacred truth,
> Your hearts with sacred fire.

The trouble is that what God has joined together we have tended to put asunder, stressing the quest of sacred truth and looking askance at the heart kindled with sacred fire. And so Christian life and service are maimed, and there is a blight upon the harvest of the Spirit.

Of course, it is right to be suspicious of emotionalism. Emotionalism can be destructive of intellectual and spiritual integrity. But it is a tragedy if we jettison emotion as well. By all means let us be clear-headed and put logic and hard thinking into the creed by which we propose to live. But it is not rational, it is simply perverse, to stifle the fire within. Jesus said that the children of darkness are sometimes wiser in their generation than the children of light. Certainly the devil knows better than to stifle emotion. He has his passionate crusaders today, millions of them; there are fierce emotions tearing the world apart. This is what Paul meant when he said that our wrestling is not against flesh and blood; it is not against any group of men or nations—Caesarism or Communism or humanism or what you will. The real warfare is deep down in an invisible realm where sinister powers of darkness stand flaming and fanatical against the dreams of Christ. And the only way to meet that demonic, mystic passion is with the fire and passion of the Lord. Perhaps the sudden uprising of the so-called Jesus movements and neo-Pentecostalism is a challenge to the church to rethink this whole matter today.

One of the great social pioneers of the nineteenth century was Josephine Butler. And her secret? Frederick Myers gave it when he said, "She introduced me to Christianity as by an inner door: not to its encumbering forms, but to its heart of flame." And even now a church, a community, an individual kindled with the flame of the love of Christ could be irresistible and make the powers of darkness tremble. It is no use, in this day when spirit forces of passionate evil have been unleashed upon the earth to make men and ideologies their instruments, it is just no use having a milk-and-water passionless religion, no good setting a tepid Christianity against a scorching paganism. We must meet the thrust of the demonic with the drive of the divine. Don't quench the fire of the Spirit! "Did not our heart burn within us?"

The two travelers by now had reached their journey's end, and their Companion was bidding them good night. He seemed to be going on further. But suddenly they realized they could not bear to let the Stranger go like this. He had cheered away their gloom and made God and hope and courage real to them again. "Don't go," they pleaded with him. "See, it is nightfall, and the stars are in the sky. Come in, and stay with us." A lovely thing, this, to happen anywhere today, and specially if you have been falling into despair about the world, or if life has hurt you personally and brought you nearer to the breaking point than you have ever told to anyone, this would be such a lovely thing to happen now. "Abide with me. Lord, I have lost heart in the struggle, and the mystery of things has deepened into darkness round my way. Help of the helpless, O abide with me!"

So their Companion of the road joined them at table that night. And there something happened—a flash of recognition that pierced their blindness. Was it some familiar gesture as he broke the bread? Was it the grace he offered? Or perhaps the sight of scars upon his hands? Suddenly they knew him. "Jesus!" they exclaimed. "You have come back to us! Then it was not defeat! And it is not all over after all. It is only just beginning. O God, be thanked, be thanked!" And he vanished out of their sight, to remain in their hearts for ever. They had hoped he would have been the deliverer of Israel. They knew now he was the conqueror of the world.

Today we can take all the disillusioned pessimistic voices shouting across the earth and clamoring in our own hearts, and shame them with the glory of Christ's resurrection. We had hoped he would be the One to redeem the race and command the world—and God has crowned that hope with certainty. If I did not know that the explosive, demonic forces which threaten ruin overreached themselves on the day of Calvary, I would get out of the pulpit and never preach again. But if the gospel means anything, it means that in the decisive hour when all the powers of hell had been mobilized for the final challenge it was turned by a divine irony to their irrevocable defeat. Of course, men and nations have their part to play. Of course, science and technology, politics, and economics are all necessary for the conservation and survival of the world. But, thank heaven, our existential decisions are not history's total resource. No! For the God of the resurrection has released into this world of frustration, corruption, and death a force that really can make all things new. The malevolent, ferocious dynamism of the spirit powers of evil has met its master. Even if Victory Day that ends the war is still to come, the decisive battle has been fought and won. This is why, properly understood, the New Testament is the most exciting book in the world. Bring the resurrection gospel to the test of the most ruthless honesty, of logic hard as nails, and it will unfold to you the creative purpose of the living God. For here is the power that will yet reclaim the wasteland of this bitter age and finally rebuild the world.

And for ourselves? That fine Cambridge scholar T. R. Glover, who wrote a famous book, "The Jesus of History," once said a striking thing about the church and its message. "I don't give tuppence for the man who goes into a pulpit to tell me where my duty lies: but I'll give all I have to the man who tells me *whence my help comes.*" And indeed, that is what matters most of all for every one of us—not where duty lies, but where our help is to come from. For I am sure I must be speaking now to some who are perplexed and sad, haunted perhaps by the aching memory of happier days now vanished, some who are battered and besieged by fierce anxiety, some whose dearest hopes have crashed in ruin, some who have lost all faith in life and love and everything, some who are ashamed or lonely or in despair. Far be it from me to minimize that trouble. But I dare not speak to you today and not make absolutely clear the Word of the Lord to you, which is this: your problem, difficult as it is, is not too difficult for the God of the resurrection to deal with. You cannot think that the terrific cosmic force which shattered death for Jesus is going to be impotent for you, or confess itself beaten on the scale of your experience. Do you not see that if this power once touches you anything is possible? You really can begin again today. This, to use T. R. Glover's word, is "whence your help comes," all the help you can ever need right on to the journey's end and beyond.

It is not my voice I would have you hear in these last moments. It is Christ's. Jesus said, "All power is given unto me in heaven and in earth." Jesus said, "I am come that they might have life, and have it more abundantly." Jesus said, "Abide in me, and I in you: without me ye can do nothing." Jesus said, "If any man open the door, I will come in."

Do you believe that? Then say, "Even so, come! Come now, Lord Jesus."

FREEDOM - FALSE AND TRUE

You see how the old Hebrew law in Exodus stood. A slave who had served his master for the legal period of six years was to be given the offer of freedom when the seventh year came round. He might take it or leave it; that was another matter. But the master was legally bound to give him the chance of it at least.

Now consider how this worked out in practice. Take two pictures. First, imagine a group of Hebrew slaves on the eve of their liberation, with the six long years behind them, years that may have felt almost like a lifetime, but now the end is in sight, and hungrily they are counting the days. "Just four days now," they are saying, "three days, two days, the last day! Tomorrow we shall be free!" trying in a bewildered, incredulous way to grasp the fabulous fact—free tomorrow! That night not a man of them tries to sleep. How could they sleep? They are singing and laughing and shouting and telling of the wonderful things waiting for them out in the wide world to which they are going back, trying to believe it is not a dream but reality—all through the night, until the first gray streaks of dawn begin to steal in, and with that they are on their feet, for the great day has come. "It's morning! We are free, thank God, we are free!" And out they go on that never-to-be-forgotten day, with the heaven above them and the open road before them.

KING FOR EVER

But now look at the other picture. Again it is the night before the day of liberation. And here is a man alone by himself, deep in troubled thought. He knows that tomorrow he is going to be given his freedom. He knows this is the hour for which he has been supposed to be waiting for years. He knows that tonight he ought to be supremely, magnificently happy. But he also knows he is not happy in the least, that indeed he is acutely miserable. For all the time one question has kept hovering in the background of his mind, a question which up till now he has been endeavoring not altogether successfully to suppress, but now at last it will not be kept down any longer, and he forces himself to face it. "Do I want my liberty? Do I really want to go out free tomorrow?" And in the very moment of asking it, he knows the answer. "No! I don't want it. I wish I had never had the chance of it." For this man during his slavery had married, and the law laid it down that anyone who went out free must go out alone. "How can I? Am I, for my freedom, to lose my dearest and best beloved? And those little ones God has given me, am I to lose them—to put their clinging arms away and go out and never see them again? And my master too, and my master's house where goodwill and kindness have always reigned, where I have been treated as a member of the family—am I to lose all that? God forbid." And so when morning comes, and the door to freedom stands wide open and the far horizon beckons, he turns his back on it. "I love my master, my wife, and my children; I will not go out free." And the master takes him and brands him and makes him his slave for ever.

So much for the Exodus passage. Now turn to the Gospel. There was a day when Jesus offered his twelve disciples their freedom. Hundreds of his followers had been deserting him; the thronging crowds had dwindled. And piercingly the thought came, "These twelve closest followers of mine—what if they should go too? Are they perhaps feeling that they have made a mistake, and wanting their freedom back?" There and then he gave them the chance, told them he was grateful for all they had done for him, but that if they wished to turn and go home now the way was open and none would prevent them. You can see them at the critical moment pondering the offer, weighing the alternatives, balancing the hardness and discipline that involvement in Christ's service meant against home and security and freedom to be their own masters, wondering "Which should it be? Are we perhaps being fools to let the chance of freedom go?" And then I see Peter—God bless him for it—breaking the spell of that strained silence and settling the matter for himself and for all the rest. "Lord, to whom shall we go? Where could we possibly go now? No one else has ever spoken to us the words of eternal life." So Peter stood there, resolute and committed. "I love my Master. I will not go out free!"

Is there some brother of Peter's here today to say the same? You pledged your troth to Christ in confirmation—was it last year or twenty years or forty years ago? You have had your taste of what Christ's service means. You have seen enough of it by this time to know how absolute is his demand. You know that giving Christ priority is going to mean a strenuous self-discipline all the way. Is it worth it? You could have your freedom for the asking, right now. Or is it with you as with the slave of Exodus and with Peter of the Gospels? "Freedom? No. I love you, Master. I cannot take it. I will not go out free!"

Look at this man in Exodus again. Three things entered into his decision, three reasons why when he took that proffered gift of freedom into his hands and examined it he decided to let it go.

First, there was this. He knew that those years in his master's house—and happy, well-ordered years they had been—had given him a new standard of living and had spoiled him for anything else. After that, the old life, with its aimlessness and insecurity and uncontrol, just would not do. He could go back to it, but he would go back a different man, and it would never satisfy him now.

You see the point. It was exactly this which bound Peter to the Master. Once any man has looked into Christ's eyes and felt the magnetism of his way of life, he is never going to be content with the secular ideals and standards that may have seemed adequate enough before Christ came. Christ has spoiled him for anything else. Thank God he has!

And yet that temptation to go out free is an experience most Christians encounter at one time or another. You know the subtle doubts that come. What if in the twentieth century it is all a mistake—the idea of Christ commitment? What if the Marxist denial of the validity of the Christian ethic, the humanist-scientific denial of the finality of the Christian revelation, and the philosophical "God is dead" denial of the reality of the transcendent and the supernatural are really true? What about all the people who are able to live apparently upright and contented lives, helpful to their neighbors and a real asset to the community, without ever darkening a church door or making any Christian profession? And there are the more intimate doubts that rear their spectral heads. What if the "happy day that fixed my choice" was simply a temporal mental aberration with a perfectly straightforward psychological explanation? What if my stumbling attempts to follow Christ are wasted time and effort? What if I have spent my strength toiling after an illusion and believing a beautiful fable? Sometimes it will even happen that a soul, under the stress and pressure of such dreary misgivings, will let the whole thing go and break away from discipleship, back to what it was before. What then? Why then, what it was before is all spoiled for it now, the old standards of value just cinders, ashes, dust. For that vision of Christ has come in between.

Think how it was with Peter and the disciples. Suppose that instead of holding fast to Jesus they had in fact chosen to go out free. Suppose that on the day he made the offer they had taken him at his word and gone back to their homes and their work in Galilee. I think I can see Peter doing it. I can see him launching the familiar boat, bending over his nets, telling himself how good it was to be back in the old place and to be done with that mad, preposterous adventure. "Now, Simon Peter my man, you are really home where you belong and where you were meant to be. No more of these ridiculous dreams of revolutionizing the world and conquering kingdoms—back in the old boat, that's best!" Do you think he could have believed it? Or was this the way of it? out on the calm waters that night, a man down on his face in the bottom of the boat, crying "O Christ, my master! Why did you ever come into my life! If you had never crossed my path, content and happy I could have been today. But now, having been with you once, I cannot bear to be without you ever. Jesus, inexorable, relentless Jesus, why must I love you so?"

Most of us must at some time have had the experience of going back to a childhood scene unvisited for years. In those far-off days how big the place seemed, vast and wide and ample! But now, returning after years, you can scarcely recognize it, so cramped it seems and small and narrow. Has the place then changed? No, but you have changed—the experiences of years have come in between. That is a parable. For once Christ has entered with his claim and challenge into your life, he has creased new standards, and by doing so has spoiled you for anything else for ever. Therefore—like the slave in Exodus, like Peter in the Gospels—"I will not go out free!"

But there was a second reason behind the decision. The Hebrew servant recognized that, if it was a question of freedom, he was actually better off where he was than he could ever be as his own master in the world outside. Suppose he had gone out friendless and alone to face the struggle for existence. What kind of freedom was that? No, the real freedom was here, in his good master's house.

Now again this is a parable. It may look like freedom outside of Christ—outside the discipline of his absolute demand, with an easygoing permissive morality—but is it in fact? The offer of freedom is the tempter's standard strategy. "Be your own master! Why should you be the slave of any cramped prohibitive ethic? Down with external regimentation, and religious scruples that impede the free exercise of your faculties." So you have latter-day prophets—in books, plays, films, television— preaching the doctrine that at all costs a man must be free to express his personality, and that if he finds anything in a moral code (any commandment of the Decalogue, for instance) standing in the way, then that restriction on his liberty of action must go. This is the characteristic sickness of modern democracy, this emphasis on expediency rather than duty, this unbridled egotistic self-expressionism, this rampant ethical individualism and irresponsibility with its slogan "Be your own master, and do as you like!" Freedom? Do not believe it. There is a catch in it. It needs no elaborate refutation from the side of religion or ethics or psychology. That offer of freedom is a cheat. It is the way not to fullness of life but to moral death.

Here are three questions worth putting to our contemporary champions of the morality of unbridled freedom. How can a man be free when he has no controlling purpose in life, no god to worship but self? "That dreary selfishness," said Whittier, "is the prison of a soul." In the vivid words of G. K. Chesterton:

> In a time of sceptic moths and cynic rusts,
> And fatted lives that of their sweetness tire,
> In a world of flying loves and fading lusts,
> It is something to be sure of a desire.

And the man who has Christ to organize his life, and to save him from meaninglessness and aimlessness, is far more of a freeman than any whose god is self. "All things are yours," Paul told his Corinthian converts, the whole world belongs to you, you are freemen of the universe. But Paul did not stop there: "All things are yours—if you are Christ's." Don't cut that text in two! If a man is to master life, let him first be mastered by Christ.

> Make me a captive, Lord,
> And then I shall be free.

The second question. How can a man be free if his deeds will not bear the light? For there is no slave driver in the world like memory, no crack of the whip like a guilty conscience. And the final question. How can a man be free when he is unable to draw out and change his way of life at will? For this is the inevitable outcome, through the inexorably binding force of habit and predisposition. The fact is—it may look like freedom outside of Christ, but the reality is bondage.

On the other hand, it may look like bondage with Christ, but the reality is freedom. Men like Peter and Paul, Bunyan and Rutherford, Bonhöffer and Martin Luther King, have been imprisoned, flogged, martyred in the service of Christ and in the very process have led captivity captive and tasted the most glorious of freedoms.

> Stone walls do not a prison make
> Nor iron bars a cage

for those who walk with Christ. This is what Jesus offers—the freedom of an integrated personality, all vagrant desires welded into one commanding purpose; the freedom of walking in the light, with nothing to hide from God or man; the freedom of joyful service, of knowing your life counts to God and man. There was a lighthouse-keeper whose days were spent on an isolated reef in the sea. "Do you not feel like a prisoner out here?" a visitor one day asked him. Swift as a flash came the answer, "Not since I saved my first man!" It is immensely significant that the man in the New Testament whose chosen name for himself was "the bondslave of Christ" was the same man who was always singing about "the glorious liberty of the children of God." The bondslave, the glorious liberty—that is the essential paradox of Christianity. And who would go back from that for any dingy, relativistic ethic? Stand fast in Christ! Any other dream of authentic existence will not come true. "Lord, to whom shall we go? Thou hast the words of eternal life."

We have now seen two reasons for the decision of the Hebrew slave and of Peter in the Gospel. But in the long run it was the third reason that was the determining factor. The final reason for both of them was this: "I love my master."

This is the unanswerable argument. No one can speak of this without the risk of becoming autobiographical. Let me put it like this. The reason why the Christian faith holds me is not that I am ignoring the difficulties which can be brought against it by the scientist, the historian, the psychologist, the secularist. It is not that I am seeking to minimize the strength of the case of the skeptic and the agnostic. It is not that I have not felt keenly in my own mind and heart the force and cogency of some of the arguments of those who write books objecting to Christian belief. In point of fact, I could mention difficulties of my own about the faith which would make all these other objections look like child's play: this above all—that it is so immensely improbable, so overwhelmingly incredible that any sinning, stumbling nature, my own or anyone else's, should ever be caught up and transfigured into the fullness of life so confidently promised in the New Testament. How can that miracle ever be? I have listened to the contemporary objections to the faith and can add others of my own. But what does it add up to when the love of God in Christ goes smiting through them all? What does it amount to when my own heart keeps crying, "Lord, to who can I go but unto thee?" All these other voices are only fumbling, guessing. This voice of Jesus is certainty, conviction, the way, the truth, the life, the crowning uttermost reality. "I love my master," said the Hebrew slave. "I love my Master," said Peter. It is the final argument.

Late on that last night in a Hebrew home I can see the master going to his servant to say good-bye and to wish him well for the journey on the morrow. He delivers to him the signed document which proclaims his freedom. I see the slave taking it with a trembling hand and reading it. "To all whom it may concern. This is to certify that Reuben, having served me faithfully for six years, is now made free. Given under my hand and seal, in Jerusalem, this first day of the first month of the tenth year of King Solomon. Signed—Joseph ben Judah." And the man who has been reading looks up, and now there are tears in his eyes. "Take it back," he begs, "I don't want it. Master, I love you. See, I refuse to accept it!" And with that he tears the precious parchment from top to bottom. "Now, master, I am yours for ever. I will never go out free." And there and then the pact till death is made.

Is it still happening today? For there is another voice now. "I have come," says Jesus to a communicant member of his church, perhaps young, perhaps not so young, "I have come to say good-bye. You have been in my company these years, but I know you have been finding it hard at times and have hankered after something different. I am going to set you free." And with that the Master puts something into the servant's hand. The servant, startled, looks at it, for this is written in blood. "This is to certify that my disciple, having walked with me from the day of his first Communion, is now made free. Signed with my own pierced hand, on the hill of Calvary. Jesus of Nazareth." And the man who has been reading it lets it drop and stands there with bowed head, not daring to look up. What is he waiting for? Man, you are free! Free to go out tomorrow with no Master to lord it over you anymore. Just think of it —no one ever to trouble you again. What are you waiting for? Then suddenly the man looks up. His pent-up feelings come pouring out. "No, not that, Jesus, anything but that! Take it back, I beg you, for God's sake take it back! To whom can I go but unto you? I love you, Master: I will never, never go out free!" And at that, very quietly, Jesus says, "Until death, then, is it?" And the answer comes, "Yes, indeed—to have and to hold, to serve and to obey, to worship and adore—until death! And beyond death, into glory."

BETTER THAN
YOUR WILDEST DREAMS

*"I bow my knees unto the Father ... that you may be able to comprehend
with all saints what is the breadth and length and depth and height;
and to know the love of Christ, which passeth knowledge,
that you might be filled with all the fullness of God."*
EPHESIANS 3:14,18,19

Frederic Myers, distinguished Victorian man of letters, was once
asked, "Suppose you could put one question to the Sphinx, with
the certainty of getting an infallible answer, what would you
ask?" Without a moment's hesitation he replied, "I'd ask, Is the
universe friendly?"

That cry represents the unspoken longing of countless hearts
today. Is creation penetrated by a controlling purpose of good?
Is there an ultimate love?

I invite you to consider one of the most luminous and emphatic
answers to that question ever given. It is enshrined in Paul's
letter to the Ephesians. The apostle is here on his knees at the
greatest intercessory prayer he ever prayed. He is wrestling
with God for the hearts and minds of his Ephesian converts.
When Jacob wrestled with the angel at Peniel, says Genesis, his
thigh was thrown out of joint. When Paul here wrestles with
God, his language, his very grammar and syntax are thrown out
of joint, so passionate is his pleading. What does he want? He
wants these people to be gripped as never before by the excitement of what God has done for them by becoming incarnate in
Jesus. He wants them to realize the transcendent, supernatural
Reality by which their ordinary lives are penetrated through and
through. And inasmuch as, speaking to them, he speaks still to
you and me, his words imply that the real reason why we are

here in church today is not custom or tradition or routine: it is something right out of this world, something better than our wildest dreams. "O that you may know," he says, "the love of Christ, which passes knowledge, its breadth, its length, its depth, its height!"

First, he says, "I want you to know *the breadth of the love of Jesus.*" The breadth of it: what is the significance of that symbolism? Surely this—that God's love in Christ is as wide as the universe; that the two arms stretched out in death's agony on the cross seem today, as you watch them, to be reaching out further and further still, until they are encircling the whole creation in a passionate embrace. It means that our facile dictum that "East is East and West is West, and never the twain shall meet" is shown once and for all at Calvary to be a lie, for in Christ that division and every other are obliterated. It means that the central fact about any man is not his nationality or race or color, not his education or illiteracy, orthodoxy or heterodoxy, not whether he is an oriental or an occidental, communist or capitalist, sophisticated or simple; the central fact about him is this—God is not ashamed to be called his God, and Christ is not ashamed to be called his brother.

> Lord, on the cross Thine arms were stretched
> To draw the nations nigh;
> O grant us then that cross to love,
> And in those arms to die.

That is the breadth of the love of Jesus. And it breaks so many man-made barriers down—things which we consider dreadfully important—simply levels them to the dust. The New Testament itself tells of that. In Jesus' day the sacred precincts of the temple of God in Jerusalem were surrounded by an enormous square, and right across that square from side to side there ran a wall, and on the wall there was a notice declaring it was strictly forbidden that any Gentile should penetrate beyond it. "Whoever, being a non-Jew, passes this point will himself be responsible for the death that overtakes him." Jesus, when he visited the temple, must have seen and read that notice. You can almost see him gazing at it, and the flush of shame upon his face. Race prejudice enshrined at the very heart of the ancestral religion! But Christ, says Paul, in this same letter to the Ephesians, broke down that wall of partition. By his death and resurrection it was smashed to atoms. There are no longer Jew and Greek, male and female, freeman and slave: you are all one in Christ.

> For the love of God is broader
> Than the measures of man's mind —

far wider in its reach and grasp than our poor fumbling imagination has ever dared to conceive, better than our wildest dreams.

"O that you may know," cries Paul, "the breadth of the love of Jesus!" Will we dare ask God to give to us something of that quality of charity, that breadth of love? Suppose we really had it, think what would happen. Think of the frictions that would be eliminated, the temperamental difficulties that would be overcome. Think of the reconciliations that would happen between those who worship God in different ways and at different altars: why, the whole ecumenical movement would suddenly pass into a new climate of hopefulness and progress. Think with what a sense of responsibility we should recognize our brotherhood with the peoples of Asia and Africa, yes, and of our own neighborhood and community. Think, too, how we should be able to get on with people whom we have never been able to get on with before, how Martha would begin to understand Mary, and how Mary would begin to appreciate Martha. Think how the whole fellowship of the church would be reborn and revitalized. The story is told that on one occasion Nelson came on board his flagship and found two of his officers quarreling, almost coming to blows, and he rebuked them with the words, "Gentlemen, there is only one enemy—France." If we who belong to Christ would realize that today there is only one enemy, the corporate sin of all of us—and only one goal, the universal kingdom of heaven—if we would build our brotherhood on that basis, broad as the love of Jesus, what a mighty force the Christian fellowship would be! Nothing in the world could stand against its impact. Surely it should not be custom or tradition that takes our lagging steps to church. Ought we not to turn in to worship joyfully and eagerly, with a gratitude beyond words for something better than our wildest dreams? "O that you may know," says Paul, "the breadth of the love of Jesus!"

Second, he says, "I want you to know *the length of the love of Jesus.*" The length of it: what is the significance of that symbolism? It means surely that this is a love which, as we say, goes all lengths, stops short at nothing, a love which will never dream of calculating less or more, but gives itself irrevocably and for ever. It means that the longest trail into the wilderness is not too long or hard for this love to travel, not even if it is as long and hard as the Via Dolorosa of the cross.

Is it not true to say that even on the human level the test of love, the only conclusive test, is the length to which it is prepared to go in action and devotion? In particular, words are no test of love. Do you remember King Lear's daughters Goneril and Regan in the play, and their loud, high-sounding protestations of affection for their father?

> Sir, I love you more than words can wield the matter;
> Dearer than eyesight, space, and liberty;
> Beyond what can be valued, rich or rare;
> As much as child e'er loved, or father found;
> Beyond all manner of so much I love you.

And all the time it was superficial and synthetic and unreal. But poor tongue-tied Cordelia, with her cry

> Unhappy that I am, I cannot heave
> My heart into my mouth —

hers was the real devotion. Words are no final test of love. The one sure test is—to what lengths will it go, in self-giving and constancy and sacrifice?

There was a day when a deputation of the citizens of Bordeaux waited on Montaigne to ask him to become their mayor. He thanked them for their courtesy and then added, "I am ready to take your affairs upon my hands, but not upon my heart or my liver." In other words, I am prepared to involve myself so far, but no further. George Eliot says of one of her characters that "he could be trusted to make any sacrifice that was not unpleasant." But all that has nothing to do with love. "Do you want me to tell you what love is?" cried Origen, the great theologian-preacher of the third century. "I will tell you now. Love is an agony."

The real test of love is the length to which it will go. It is Captain Oates of the Antarctic walking out into the blizzard to his death in order that the men he loved should not be burdened with his helpless life. It is the men of a Yorkshire coal-mine battling underground for days and nights on end through the most frightful conditions of water and mud and darkness and danger in an attempt to reach and save their trapped comrades cut off by flood and fire. It is two missionaries who lost their daughter from leprosy, and who—instead of being embittered by their loss—resolved to go back to the very place where she died and establish a leper colony. It is Kagawa of Japan telling his fellow Christians, "If you are prepared to die for it, there is nothing you cannot accomplish." It is every vicarious soul in the congregation today who is trying, in response to some inner vision of his or her own heart, to bear a burden for someone else and is glad before God of the chance of doing it.

Love's test is love's length. And if that is true on the human level, how much more true it is of the love divine all human loves excelling! Listen to John in one of the greatest sentences he ever penned. "Hereby perceive we the love of God," or rather, as his Greek might more accurately be translated, "we realize what love means by this—that God laid down his life for us." It is as though he said, "I never knew before what love really was, never grasped its meaning or its nature, thought it was just a kind of untroubled bliss, a summer's day unvisited by storm or sadness; until one day I stumbled upon a cross, saw

Someone hanging there in agony, heard him cry 'Father, forgive them,' saw the light of peace and victory in those dying eyes, then all of a sudden I knew. I knew that all I had ever thought of love before was pitifully poor and inadequate. Hereby perceive we what love means, when we see God laying down his life for us."

"I must confess," wrote Sir Philip Sidney long ago, "I never heard the old story of Percy and Douglas that I found not my heart moved more than with a trumpet." But today in this place we have something more moving by far. Can you hear the old, ever-new story of Jesus and his love without having your heart stirred more than by all the trumpets in the world? Of course it is right to be concerned—deeply and terribly concerned—about the chaos of the world. It is imperative to become involved. But our concern and our involvement are going to be not less practical and purposeful but far more so if we know and are sure that our human darkness has already, once and for all, been pierced and penetrated by a transcendent, supernatural light, more potent than our most dazzling technologies, more luminous than our brightest dreams. "O that you may know," says Paul, "the length of the love of Jesus!"

Third, says the apostle, "I want you to know *the depth of the love of Jesus.*" The depth of it; what do you think that symbolizes? Surely this—that from the heights of heaven, out of the infinite serenity of the eternal world, God in Christ came down to our level, bone of our bone and flesh of our flesh, and not only down to the level of humanity at its noblest and best, the vanguard leaders of mankind's march across the centuries, heroes, saints, apostles, martyrs; but far, far lower than that, down into the inferno of ugliness and shame that the sins of men create; down, as the psalmist puts it, to the fearful pit and the miry clay—so that when you stand gazing at Calvary there is something which assures you, not only that the top of that redeeming cross reaches up to heaven, not only that the two arms of it embrace the whole wide world, but also that the shaft of it reaches down to the abyss, down to every poor pathetic creature who has ever made his bed in hell. The depth of the love of Jesus!

No wonder friend and foe alike have stood amazed at that. There was a man in the second century called Celsus, a brilliant and redoubtable skeptic, who lashed the church with merciless scorn and satire, and it was this that Celsus fixed on as the finally discrediting thing about the new religion—the depth to which Christ sank. "Jesus think," he said in effect, "think of the people this Jesus mixed with, the kind of people with whom he felt most at home. Why, you and I would not have gone near them for worlds!" And there, of course, Celsus was just reviving an earlier criticism. "Friend of publicans and sinners," they sneered disdainfully as the Man of Nazareth passed down the streets. And then no doubt they would talk. "What a pity that he should have lowered himself like this! He might have done something worthwhile if only he had looked after his reputation better. He might have been a real religious force in Judaism and beyond. But now—well, you know how it is—a man is recognized by the company he keeps, and of course that finishes him!" And then another would take up the tale. "Yes," he would say, "and did you hear about last night? It was outside Zacchaeus's house. You know the kind of man he is—the less said about his character the better. All these taxgatherers are alike, renegades, rogues, extortioners. Well, I was passing his house, and there were people going in—it was rumored they were Zacchaeus's friends, invited to a supper party to meet this Jesus; so I stood and watched, and I tell you the very dregs of the town were there, foul things that creep about under cover of the dark. By and by Jesus came and made as though to enter, and I touched him on the arm as he passed and said, 'Don't go in there! It is not safe, the company is noxious, it is not worth it!' But he just looked at me and said, 'The Son of Man is come to seek and to save,' and his face was shining, and he went in, and the doors were shut." And of course the group listening to the story would lift up their hands in horror. "The utter abasement of it!" they would cry, "the lowering, the degradation, the depth of it!" But look, today, across the years, we have taken that very gibe and turned it into a glory. "O the depth of the love of Christ!" we cry.

> Down beneath the shame and loss
> Sinks the plummet of the cross.
> Never yet abyss was found
> Deeper than Thy love can sound.

I would not dare to say that even Judas was irretrievably lost and ruined.

In the village churchyard at Grasmere, not far from Wordsworth's tomb, there is the grave of poor Hartley Coleridge, a man of wayward life, with great gifts thwarted by his own frailty, and by what he himself described as "the woeful impotence of weak resolve." On the stone that bears his name are carved the haunting words of the Litany, "By Thy cross and passion, good Lord, deliver us"; just as though the sadly wasted life had cast itself at the last out of the depths upon the Rock of Ages.

Where should you, I, any of us, be today if it were not for the depth of the love of Jesus? "Out of the depths have I cried unto thee, O Lord." I know what that means. I have been there. And so have you—the day of feeling baffled and defeated and spiritually bankrupt and alone. Our whole world is there, our bewildered war-torn world. "Do profundis clamavi." When we sing the great words of Psalm 130—

> Lord, from the depths to Thee I cried,
> My voice, Lord, do Thou hear—

are we realizing how intimately and factually our own condition is mirrored here? "My soul waiteth for the Lord more than they that watch for the morning; I say, more than they that watch for the morning." No one ever waited for God like that in vain. No cry from the depths was ever unanswered. Deep as your need is, the grace of Christ is deeper far, and it is on that level of sheer desperate need that his greatest work is done. For always, even at the lowest deeps, "underneath are the everlasting arms." This is the divine answer to the human dilemma, and it is better, far better, than our wildest dreams. "O that you may know," says Paul, "the depth of the love of Jesus!"

Finally, says Paul, "I want you to know *the height of the love of Jesus.*" The height of it—what do you think that symbolizes? Surely this—that Christ has opened to us the gates of highest heaven, that he has taken our lowly life and bound it with chains of gold about the feet of God. "Behold," cries John, "what manner of love the Father hath bestowed upon us," or rather, for that hardly does justice to the original, "behold, what an unearthly love it is, that we should be called the sons of God." Then there comes a sudden shout, "And so we are!" Sons of God, and so we are! That is the height of the love of Jesus: that you and I, knowing ourselves as we are, "frail children of dust, and feeble as frail," with natures that are a strange jumble of conflicting emotions and desperately difficult instincts, poor pathetic bunglers making a sorry tangle of our life, feeling sometimes that no one cares, and what does it matter, and the game is almost up—that we, knowing ourselves so well, should be lifted up and treated by Christ on that level, sons and daughters of God! If that does not heal us of our self despising, nothing will: if that cannot turn our defeatism to victory, nothing can.

And there is more in it even than that. That is not the crowning achievement of the height of the love of Jesus. For do you remember how John goes on? "Beloved, now are we the sons of God; and it doth not yet appear what we shall be: but we know that, when He shall appear, we shall be like him; for we shall see him as he is." But that is incredible! I can't believe it. Or rather, I ought to say, if it were not in the Word of God it would be incredible. But here it stands: so I must learn to believe it. Not like saints, not like angels—like Christ himself! Does it not take your breath away to realize that that, nothing less, is what God is aiming at in you and me—these poor broken characters of ours to be like Christ's character, these feeble wills to be like Christ's will, these stained and sullied souls to be like Christ's soul? That is the measure of our destiny—and some we loved have entered on it already. That is the height of the love of Jesus.

> He only could unlock the gate
> Of heaven, and let us in.
> O dearly, dearly has He loved!

So today we celebrate the one basic certainty of life, the transcendent, supernatural reality of a love by which our little lives are penetrated through and through. But Paul is careful to remind us that we can never truly comprehend it in isolation. It must be, he says, "with all the saints," that is, in the reinforcing fellowship of the people of God, their faith and vision confirming ours, the witness of the Christian centuries and the universal church contributing to the conviction kindled by the Holy Spirit in our hearts. Why go to church? Because we have something to celebrate which is really better than our wildest dreams. And so we turn our faces to the road again, with Christ's dear friendly voice ringing in our ears, with his kind touch upon our hand, the light of his beloved presence in our hearts, and on our lips the cry—

> Just as I am, of that free love
> The breadth, length, depth, and height to prove,
> Here for a season, then above,
>   O Lamb of God, I come.

It is all yours for the taking now. O Lamb of God, I come!

WHAT LACK I YET?

"Good Master, what shall I do that I may inherit eternal life?"
MARK 10:17

There are some Scripture characters who have been maligned by generations of commentators, and this young ruler is one of them. It has become quite customary to look down on him. A poor, feeble sort of creature surely, to have been so near the kingdom and yet to have stayed outside! Here was a man, told on Christ's infallible authority the one right thing to do; how astonishing that he should not have gone and done it at once! The tacit assumption is that if we had been in his shoes there would have been a very different story to tell. The man was obviously more than a little of a coward and poltroon. This is a frequent assessment today.

Of course it is gratuitously wrong. I want to champion this man against his denigration by pious homilists with a leaning toward the obvious and a propensity for pointing the moral. No shilly-shallying timeserver this; he was a man with ideals and a soul. And as for the assumption that we should have acted differently, are we so sure? I think I might have done just the same.

For what are the facts? Here at any rate are two facts to keep in view. On the one hand, the demand Christ made on this man was absolutely astounding—bordering, many would say, on the preposterous. And on the other hand, Jesus to this man was not Son of God; he was simply a new prophet, with an exciting message, a magnetic personality, and eyes that gripped you when you spoke to him—certainly not the Christ of the Apostles' Creed. Are we sure our reaction would have been so utterly different? Let him among us who has never refused Christ anything cast the first stone.

So it is from this that we must begin: *the reassessment of a character.* Let us try to see this man in truer perspective. I call your attention to certain points in his favor too often overlooked. First, his courage. Luke designates him a "ruler." That is, he belongs to the ruling class to which Jesus and all his works were anathema: any member of that class seen consorting with the despised Nazarene might well be blacklisted and ostracized forthwith. That may have been why Nicodemus, who belonged to the same stratum of society, went to see Jesus by night, discreetly waiting for the darkness to cover his tracks. But this man was different. He did not skulk in the gloaming. He came to Christ in broad noonday. If they chose to record in the minutes of their executive committees an official censure of his deed, let them go ahead and do it. He was not going to be dictated to. Even today it takes some fortitude to defy the conventions of a social set. Must we not admit that there is too much timid conformity among Christians, too little heroic holiness? So let us set it down to this man's credit—his courage.

Besides that, there was his impetuosity. "He came running," says the evangelist. That, of course, might have seemed remarkably undignified. Onlookers would watch astonished, wondering "Now what can have happened to him?" But this, he knew, was possibly his one chance of a heart-to-heart talk with Jesus, and there was Jesus moving further and further down the road, probably right out of his life for ever. Somehow he could not bear to lose the fleeting opportunity. Let others stand upon their dignity if they chose! "He came running." There is far too much fear of unconventionality in Christian ranks today, too much stereotyped routine. Here all that was thrown to the winds. Set that down to his credit, his impetuosity.

Mark, further, his humility. "He knelt to Jesus," says the evangelist. Thank God, his status in the establishment had not made him arrogant and consequential. He fell down on his knees in the road. The story of it might become the jest next day of every wayside tavern; he did not care. Nor did it concern him that the sinister eyes of Caiaphas' secret police might be watching. For here was Jesus, and Jesus was so different from all their rabbinic notabilities and priestly hierarchy. He knelt in the dust before him. No trace of pride or pomposity here! There is no greater contradiction of terms than a pompous Christian. Of all deadly sins, pride is probably the deadliest. Set that down on the credit side, his humility.

Finally, there was his sincerity. He was not coming to Jesus with logical puzzles, dialectical conundrums, pious jargon. "Good Master, what must I do for life? I feel so thwarted, unhappy, unfulfilled. And you, Jesus, who have clearly found the secret of authentic existence, tell me what is wrong! What must I do for life?" At least he was asking the right question. He was right down at fundamentals. We know full well in our own hearts how often there can be a film of unreality even over religious professions, and how reluctant sometimes we are to face the basic issues. But nothing of that here! Add this to his credit—his sincerity.

So much for the reassessment of a character. Note now, in the second place, *the restlessness of a frustrated life.* For here was a man driven to Christ not so much by a consciousness of sin as by a sense of incompleteness. "What lack I yet?" He was not an Augustine, with a fiercely accusing conscience. He was not a John Bunyan, feeling miserably he had committed the sin against the Holy Ghost. No. It was that strange nagging sense of emptiness, that inner desolate feeling of missing the mark.

I have no doubt there were moods of a different kind. There were days when a voice within him said, "Man, why can't you be content with what you have? There are thousands who would gladly change places with you tomorrow—and you know it. You are a fool not to accept your good fortune and keep quiet!" But he could not help it. The years were passing, drifting aimlessly away. Surely God has something more meaningful for me than this drab conventional security, this dull tedious conformity. It is suffocating me. I must break its tyranny. I must get out!" And that is what drove him to Jesus.

I am not suggesting, of course, that this is the only or even the most frequent way. There are so many different roads leading toward the kingdom of God. Some are brought there by a mother's prayers; some through the worship of the church; some through serving the lonely and the wretched for the love of Christ. Some there are who are driven to it because suffering and sorrow have desolated them, and their broken hearts need healing. "I was not persuaded into religion," said William Cowper, "I was scourged into it." But here was a man traveling the other road, cast upon Jesus by a sense of incompleteness. "What must I do? Something is needed to make life significant for me. But, Lord, what is it? What lack I yet?"

It is the road that many, consciously or unconsciously, are traveling still. And it can so easily lead—that stinging frustrated sense of missing the mark in life—to unhappy psychological repercussions, neurosis and depression, and even to the dangerous recklessness of complete defeatism. But it does not need to lead to that. It can lead, as it did here, to Christ.

> I sometimes think if I could spend
> One hour alone with Thee,
> My human heart would come again
> From Thy divinity.

Now when you watch what happened here, the next turn of the narrative might seem surprising. For it has to do with *the relevance of the commandments.* Jesus, faced with this young man's urgent quest, began with the Decalogue. "You know the commandments"—one, two, three, tabulating them. Whereupon, looking on Jesus with level, steady eyes, he answered, "All these have I kept from my youth." How undeniably noble, and yet how terribly naïve!

Noble, yes, certainly. For it gives the lie to that falsely romantic view of sin that glamorizes the prodigal son, suggesting that somehow he was a better man than he could possibly have been if he had never left home and never got splashed with mud and misery. I protest against the frothy, unintelligent sentimentalizing in novels, films, plays, and indeed in contemporary society—the romanticizing of what the Word of God says is just common sin. It is high time we stopped being browbeaten by the prestige of certain literary and social reputations and the vogue of dubious, high-pressure methods in advertisement and entertainment, time we nailed down the clever, twisted tampering with the law of God, and labeled it pernicious and sacrilegious.

Here was this man who could say sincerely, "All these commandments I have kept from my youth." It was then, says the narrative, that "Jesus looking on him loved him."

"All these have I kept," undeniably noble—yes. But also, in a sense, curiously naïve. For who can perfectly keep the commandments—specially Christ's own searching, drastic heightening of the commandments written into the Sermon on the Mount? Take even the first commandment, "Thou shalt have no other gods before me." How did this young man stand to that? No rival to God? What about his possessions, his social status, his security? Were there no dear idols there usurping the throne divine? Indeed, can any of us say, All these I have kept? And even if we could say it, which obviously we cannot, would that be how life eternal is to be won? Is not the whole function of the commandments precisely this—to reveal to us our helplessness, and by so doing to lead us right away beyond laws to the grace that reconciles and humbles and makes new?

"Jesus, looking on him, loved him." But the next words show how unsentimental and searching was that love. For the next words confront us with *the radicalness of the divine demand.* "One thing you need: go, sell all you have, give to the poor, and you will have treasure in heaven, and come, take up the cross and follow me."

Perhaps our first instinct may be to say that this at any rate cannot be meant to apply to us, even in a modified form. But we should not be too quick with such a reaction. Surely the quite radical attitude of Jesus to possessions—not only here but all through the Gospels, where again and again he speaks not necessarily of the sinfulness of affluence, but certainly of its dangers alike for society and for the individual, not indeed condemning the rich man, but certainly deeply concerned for him with such a handicap to his spiritual life and growth in grace—this radical attitude of Jesus challenges us to reassess our possessions and position, and everything we are inclined to take for granted, in the light of the absolutely appalling needs of millions of our fellow creatures for whom Christ died every whit as much as he died for us, and in whose sufferings and starvation Christ himself is suffering and starving today. It challenges us in the church to recognize that the very best we may ever have given to God in the way of stewardship and tithing and sacrificial giving is in the last resort poor and paltry and not worth mentioning compared with what God has given to us. That was the trouble here in the story. And that is often the trouble today.

But of course it may be something different which stands in the way of commitment to God's will. It may, for instance, be personal ambition and the will to self-determination. Or it may be complacency, censoriousness, the refusal to forgive. It may be a rigid traditionalism that dislikes any change and refuses the challenges and opportunities of a revolutionary age. It may be some secretly besetting sin. In every case, it is that unsurrendered area of life on which Christ fixes lovingly but inexorably, thrusting it upon our vision, and then waits to see what we will do.

Here in the story the radicalness of the divine demand leads on to *the refusal of the light*. The treatment proved too radical. The man is taken aback. The light has gone out of his eyes, the ardor out of his spirit. He cannot look Jesus in the face anymore. He speaks no further word. A moment he lingers there, the picture of dejection, then turns and goes away.

I can see Christ gazing after him, dreadfully disappointed, hurt to the heart to see a soul so near the kingdom yet thwarting God's will to save. "He went away sorrowful," says the evangelist, and I reckon he left behind him an even more sorrowful Christ.

Suppose he had done what Jesus suggested. Let us picture it. He sold his possessions, gave to the poor, left his comfortable existence, and joined the disciples. He was welcomed as a new recruit, given the right hand of fellowship by Peter and Andrew and John, rose every morning for another day of wonderful fellowship with Jesus, began excitingly to discover the truth of that word of the Master's, "You shall have treasure in heaven." Within a month he was looking back on the old encumbered possessive life with immense relief that it was done, "How could I have endured it so long?" Within a year he had learned the blessed truth behind the words "Whom the Lord loveth he chasteneth, and scourgeth every son whom he receiveth"; the truth of which Francis Thompson was to tell:

> All which I took from thee I did but take,
>   Not for thy harms,
> But just that thou might'st seek it in My arms;

the truth of which George Matheson sang:

> I lay in dust life's glory dead,
> And from the ground there blossoms red
>   Life —

not some pale, thin, devitalized existence, but real red throbbing life—the very thing which all his days this man had been seeking. Within twenty years, he was helping Paul to carry the fiery cross from East to West and set the world ablaze, and his story was going down in Scripture, his name in the glorious company of the apostles. What a shining biography!

It is not here. "He went away sorrowful."

But wait. Is it not possibly here after all? Some hint of it at least? May we not go beyond the Gospel narrative and add a final chapter? I shall call it *the return of the wanderer*. For is there not a ray, a gleam of hope in that word "sorrowful"? Not resentful. Not indignant. Not blazing with offended pride. Sorrowful. That sorrow of his is like a morning star across the darkness. I begin to hope he really did come back.

Perhaps it was not for some considerable time. Perhaps not until the earthly ministry of Jesus was over. Perhaps not until he had stood on the edge of the crowd at Calvary and watched the end and heard the shout of victory with which the conquering spirit on the cross went home to God. Perhaps not until he had been haunted for years by what he had seen there, haunted by the life he had refused, haunted by the pleading eyes of Jesus.

But it would be so lovely to be allowed to think that in the end he did return. Listen to this extract from the records of the early church in Jerusalem, in the days when the tide of the Christian faith was sweeping the land, "As many as were possessors of lands or houses sold them, and brought the prices of the things that were sold, and laid them down at the apostles' feet: and distribution was made to every man according to his need." Is this a clue? I wonder. The writer of Acts continues, "Joses, surnamed Barnabas (which is, being interpreted, The son of consolation), a Levite, of the country of Cyprus, having land, sold it, and brought the money, and laid it at the apostles' feet." I wonder—was the rich young ruler Barnabas? Or if not, was this at any rate the way he took? Is this the real end of the story—an end that was a beginning—the command of Jesus at long last obeyed, and obeyed with magnificent abandon?

Conjecture? Be that as it may, here I give you something which is not conjecture, but fact: a man may go away from Jesus sorrowful and be haunted and return.

It is told that there was a day when young Count Zinzendorf, a name destined to be for ever honored in the annals of Christendom, was burning some old unwanted documents, scraps of parchment and paper, and there was one piece that escaped the flames. He poked it back into the fire, but somehow obstinately it refused to burn. Idly he took it up, and saw there was something written on it. The words he read were these:

O let us in Thy nail-prints see
Our calling and election free.

Suddenly he knew this was God speaking to him, challenging him to follow Christ and serve him with the passion of his life. And I say today, once hear the call of God in Jesus, and you cannot forget it. You cannot blot it out as though it had never been. *The scrap of paper won't burn.* It has your name on it, and Christ's, and it is the Spirit of God that has joined these names together.

> O let *me* in Thy nail-prints see
> *My* calling and election free —

Jesus, dear master, my Lord and God for ever.

THE STRANGE
STRATEGY OF GOD

"The Lord said to Gideon, 'The people with you are too many.'
Twenty-two thousand returned, and ten thousand remained.
And the Lord said to Gideon, 'The people are still too many;
take them down to the water and I will test them for you there.'
He retained the three hundred men;
and the camp of Midian was below him in the valley."
JUDGES 7:2,3,4,8 (RSV)

This is one of Scripture's most searching pages. For the church
and for all of us who profess and call ourselves Christians, this
old story is testing and radical. God looked at the thirty-two
thousand volunteers who had offered their services. "No," God
said, "too many by far! Reduce them." And it was done. Then
God looked at the remaining ten thousand and said, "Still too
many! Reduce them." And again it was done. Then God looked
at the three hundred and said, "Now, Gideon, there are your
men. Quick, march!" For all soldiers of the King of kings,
claiming to march beneath the banner of the cross, this is one of
Scripture's probing, piercing pages; a vivid commentary on the
saying of the epistle to the Hebrews, "The word of God is quick,
and powerful, and sharper than any two-edged sword, a discerner
of the thoughts and intents of the heart."

But let us start at the beginning. The first thing to be noticed
is this—as soon as Gideon sent his fiery cross through the tribes,
thirty-two thousand responded to its summons.

You must remember that at the time Israel was a broken
nation, her spirit cowed and crushed and dead, not a sign of life
in her. But as soon as one man, braver than the rest, stood up and
gave a strong lead, from every corner of the land they came, and

soon the cry was echoing round the countryside, "The sword of the Lord and of Gideon!" One decisive lead was all they were needing.

It is like this still in our modern society. At any given moment, there are thousands of people ready to stand up and be counted on the side of righteousness—if only someone would give them a lead. Look at the chaotic welter of the world today. O for some Gideon to arise! He would need to be an international figure, and he would have to be truly a man of the spirit, but granted this, what might he not achieve? Perhaps God has him somewhere in the background even now. Perhaps at the appointed time he will come forth and give the signal. Who can tell?

But in point of fact we have no need to wait on perhaps and peradventure. We have him right now—a greater than Gideon, the living contemporary Christ, the desire of all nations, the answer to all men's dreams, the one unflickering light of this dark world, the Captain of our salvation. And this is our irrefragable hope and confidence.

There is a supplementary question implicit here. Do you not think that, under Christ, you might be giving a lead to someone here and now? Is this not the duty of active witness to which our Christian calling commits us? You know how, in singing, there are hundreds of people who can take up a tune, but who could not possibly start it, someone has to begin it, to give the lead, and then they can follow and join in. It is exactly the same in this matter of Christian influence. Do realize there is someone, unknown to you perhaps, looking to you at this moment, influenced by you, depending on the kind of lead you give. There is an extraordinary amount of spiritual hunger today in the most unlikely places. And every Christian is a potential transmitter of the very life of Christ. You are bound in honor not to fail.

So Gideon gave the lead, and raised the brave old battered standard of Israel, and thirty-two thousand came. The leader himself was understandably elated at the response. "Thirty-two battalions overnight—how marvelous! Now at last we can take the field against our Midianite oppressors. Now at long last we can throw off our chains and slavery!"

The God spoke. "Wait a moment, Gideon, wait a moment! That army of yours—there is only one thing wrong with it. It is far too big!" Can you imagine the man's astonishment? "Too big? And I was just thinking how fine it would be if I could raise another half-dozen battalions!" "It is too big," said God, "you must thin them out."

Why? What was the reason? The narrative itself indicated a variety of reasons.

The first is given in verse two, "Lest Israel vaunt themselves against me, saying, my own hand has saved me." In other words, their confidence was to be not in numbers or equipment or anything of the kind. The reduction of the host was to prove that God's, and not man's, was the victory.

Here, then, is the question we have to face. Where is the church's confidence based today? Is it in the worldwide organization, the machinery of good works, the hoarded venerable traditions, the prestige of general assemblies, the modern, much publicized strategies and experiments, the involvement in the world, the public relations, and the use of the most up-to-date mass media for the propagation of the faith? All that has a part to play certainly, a really important part. But is that our basic confidence as a church? Or is it not that at all, but the one asset we possess which gives us any right to exist as a church, namely Christ, and Christ alone?

And what of ourselves, in this difficult, precarious life? What are we looking to, to bring us through the unknown years ahead? Our foresight, our planning, our intelligence and independence and perspicacity, our technological know-how, our conscious self-sufficiency? But can we not see that all that human self-confidence is really pathetically naïve and nonsensical? It is such a dreadfully poor second best compared with the transcendent equipment we are offered. "Not by might, nor by power, but by my Spirit, saith the Lord."

A second reason for the reduction of Gideon's army is given in verse three, "Whosoever is fearful and afraid, let him return." In other words, there were men who should not have been there at all. It was a mere gust of emotion that had swept them in. It was so good to see the old flag flying again, good to be in with this surging crowd, good to have found a leader! What they did not ask, what in fact they had never thought of asking was, Where is he likely to lead us? What about Midian? What about the pains and privations of the field? And when it came to that, when it was made plain to them that the whole purpose of the exercise came down at last to that portentous prospect; why, they were gone, before Gideon could even give them a valedictory speech. Twenty-two thousand of them, gone!

Turn the pages of scripture to the Gospels, and you see it all repeated. How the crowds flocked to Jesus, the new Gideon, when the standard was first raised in Galilee! His personality and his teaching fascinated them. "Never man spoke like this Man." This was new. This was a thrill they had never experienced before. This was potential leadership at its highest. This was the way to "the kingdoms of this world and the glory of them." "Lord, we will follow thee whithersoever thou goest!" Of course we will! But they had not asked, Where is he likely to lead us? And then one day Jesus held up before them an appalling thing—a gallows-tree, a cross, stark and fierce and dreadful. "Will you follow me now?" One day he confronted them with an imperious moral absolute that challenged all their dingy relativities and ethical vacillations and concessions. "Will you follow me now?" The Son of God goes forth not to carnival or debate—the Son of God goes forth to war. "Will you follow me now?"

And with that, they were stammering out their apologies. "We did not know, we had not bargained for this. This does change the aspect of things. We must have time to reconsider. Perhaps we shall be back later, but meanwhile, good-bye Jesus, good-bye," and next moment they were hurrying away. "We are well out of that," they told themselves. "What a preposterous program! And what a blessing we came out of it before it was too late!" And they looked back to where that solitary Figure stood. "I have trodden the winepress alone, and of the people there was none with me."

It happened in Gideon's day. It happened in Jesus' day. Is it perhaps happening now? Suppose our own branch of the church had to face the same kind of trial which the church of God in China or in eastern Europe has been called upon to meet; suppose God were to give us a dose of the same strong medicine, involving the question how far to go with the powers that be and where to dig in and say, "Thus far and no further," whatever the consequences—how would our church react? This test may indeed be coming in the hidden years ahead. What if the era of secular indifference to the Christian faith should lead on to a period of open hostility and antagonism? How should we react? Bring it nearer home. Suppose I knew that tomorrow I should have to choose between Christ and persecution, actual physical persecution, or even suppose my witness as a Christian were to elicit the frigid amusement of my social set, what would the effect be? Might I be tempted to recant? Or would I cry "Get behind me, Satan! Take everything else, but Christ you shall not take"? It is at least worth pondering the question.

Come back to Gideon and his army. The third reason why all those thousands were sent home is now clear: God saw they were not an asset to the cause—they were a liability. Their heart was not in it. They would reduce the temperature of the whole enterprise. They would have a dispiriting and dampening influence on all the rest.

And this is Christ's problem too. It has always been the problem—certainly since Constantine in the fourth century made Christianity official, with the blessing of the establishment. This is the problem: the nominal disciples who retard the whole adventure, signing on without meaning very much by it, thus causing the chariot wheels of the kingdom to drag, and the whole ongoing mission and evangelism of the church to lose momentum.

I reckon that the Midianites, if they had spies out, knew that it was positively to their advantage that the Israelite army had grown so large; for as long as those doubtful elements were there, Gideon would not dare to make the pace too hot.

And that is precisely what certain anti-Christian elements in society delight in today. For they have their spies out, assessing the Christian faith. They know that the more nominal adherents Christianity has, the more its accredited representatives play about with "God is dead" theologies and contingent, equivocal ethics, the more diluted the intensity of conviction and the more hesitant and apologetic the note of the supernatural—the less likely is the church to make any serious impact. The less likely is it that any sparks will fly or anyone catch fire. And of course the world gloats.

But now underlying all this, one more reason for the reduction of Gideon's host emerges from the story: God's strategy does not depend on numbers. We count heads. God does not. God counts hearts. We talk about extending the kingdom, producing more disciples: God aims at intensifying the kingdom and producing better disciples. We talk about High Church, Low Church, Broad Church, but what God wants to see is the Deep Church. Do not give me the big ecclesiastical battalions, cried John Wesley, "give me a hundred men who fear nothing but sin and love nothing but God, and I will shake the gates of hell!" Where did Wesley learn that attitude? Surely from his royal master Jesus, who in the parable of the leaven—a substance small, insignificant, quantitatively unimpressive, but immensely vital—made clear once for all the divine strategy of his world campaign. What that strategy means is this, that Christ would rather any day have a poor 5 percent minority of resolute souls to work with, than a great 95 percent majority unconvinced and pliable in their allegiance.

How in point of historical fact did Christ's church, in the great days after Pentecost, sweep the Mediterranean world? Not because they were mighty and many and influential, not because they numbered their legions by scores of thousands—nothing of the kind—but simply because the few that there were of them were dead sure of Christ, believing in his passion and resurrection and eternal Lordship, and believing not vaguely and conventionally, as we so often do today, but believing with intensity and passion, for they were experiencing his living presence with them every day and recognized it as literally the most important fact in all the world.

This was the miracle of Pentecost. And we are needing nothing short of a new Pentecost to recreate that attitude within us. May God grant it to us soon!

Come back to Gideon and his army. Twenty-two thousand departed, ten thousand remained. I imagine Gideon saying to himself, "Well, we are surely ready for action now. We cannot possibly be reduced further. This is the absolute minimum." But God said, "Do not be so sure, my friend, not quite so sure! I am going to test them once again."

And so there ensued that strange discriminating process at the river. It is a marvelously vivid story. When they reached the water, the great bulk of them flung themselves down to drink, heeding not the possibility of an ambush, took off their helmets, slackened their belts, removed their equipment, forgetting they were on campaign and that at any moment the foe might be upon them. But there were a few, the real soldier spirits, who—as the writer of Judges tells—simply lapped up a few handfuls of water, never once relaxing vigilance, never once taking their eyes off Gideon their leader, ready to spring to attention in an instant. And God, setting aside all the others, singled out that eager, disciplined three hundred. "There," said God to Gideon, "there are your men!"

Do you catch the meaning? The three hundred were chosen, not because they were heroes, but because even while they paused to drink the water their eyes were fixed on Gideon; because they were so dead keen on the business in hand that not for one moment would they take their eyes off their leader!

And today when Christ's campaign is on, when the enemy now is not Midian, not Caesarism nor Communism, not agnosticism nor apathy, but foes more sinister and subtle by far, unseen principalities and powers, all the lurking, ambushed things that wait for our unguarded hours, there is only one salvation—up with your eyes to Christ! For a Greater than Gideon is here. And like a star across the blackest night of my bewilderment and doubt and temptation shines for me the blessed and beloved face of Jesus. This is the one fact in life of which I am utterly and for ever sure: that if Jesus is not the clue to history there is no clue anywhere, that he is Lord of the world and Lord of my life too. Up with your eyes to Christ! And you will be there when the gallant three hundred smash Midian in the morning.

"Well," someone may say to me, "that may be all very true. But it cannot be like that for me. For I am one of the crowd who left the Leader and deserted the campaign. I have taken the easy compromising way and failed my Savior. So there is not much comfort in this old story for me!" Is there not? Just wait a moment. Here is the last touch in the narrative—it is too often overlooked. When Gideon's first decisive battle had been won, all those others came back. And Gideon welcomed them. "Oh," you say, "not very heroic to rejoin the standard then!" Yes, it was; for though the decisive battle was over, there was still a long way to the Victory Day that was to end the war, and there were other battles to be fought and won. They came back, and Gideon was glad to welcome them.

It is the heart of the faith, that Christ's decisive battle has been won. You were not there to help, nor was I; no one was there to help, not three hundred, not even three. For even his chosen disciples failed him at the end. It was then, in the solitude of Calvary, that the victory was achieved, once for all, when he broke the powers of darkness, lifted the burden of the world on to his own shoulders, and turned the tide of the campaign. The decisive battle—finished. But now the crucial question. Am I coming back? He says he wants me and will welcome me. "Not very heroic," you say, "to rejoin the standard now!" Yes, it is; for though the decisive battle is finished and complete, there is still a long campaign before the Victory Day that is to end the war, and there are other combats to be fought and won. Are you coming in? He will be so glad to welcome you.

Here is the kind of message I suggest we should send to our Commander today: "O Jesus, I have been such a disappointment to you and to myself! I have broken away from your ranks. I have not kept step with your will and plan. O Christ, forgive me! I want to join up again today. I long to be a better kind of Christian. I know you are marching on across the ages, and I want you to give me the strength to follow you. Lord, for your tender mercies's sake, accept me as now into your hands I give myself, body, soul, and spirit in total commitment, to serve your cause more faithfully—Lord, for your tender mercies's sake!"

THE HIGHER REALISM

"David encouraged himself in the Lord his God."
I SAMUEL 30:6

There is a strange legend which describes how once upon a time God, perceiving that the devil had too many weapons in his armory, decided that they should be reduced to one. The devil was to be allowed to choose which one of all his weapons he would keep, what single power over men he would retain, when all the rest were given up. He resolved to retain as his one weapon the power of discouragement: for, said he, "If only I can persuade men and women to be thoroughly discouraged, they will make no further moral effort, and then I shall be enthroned in their lives."

Now most of us, I have no doubt, have had to face at one time or another this particular private devil of discouragement. There may be some few fortunate spirits who can honestly say that they have never known what it meant to feel downhearted or depressed, but for most of us, there would be a different story to tell.

And the causes of this condition are legion. For example, it may be discouragement about the way the world is going that weighs heavily upon the mind. What with one economic crisis following another, the depersonalizing effects of a machine-made culture, the industrial unrest, the crime wave, the crude and senseless vandalism, the overhanging threat of nuclear catastrophe—where are we to turn? The dismal tale of hopes frustrated seems to drag on interminably, and dreams once shining and enchanting begin to look tarnished and dingy and ridiculous. "Say not," cried the poet, foreseeing this danger,

> Say not, the struggle nought availeth,
>   The labour and the wounds are vain,
>   The enemy faints not, nor faileth,
>   And as things have been they remain.

But how can we help saying it in times like these?

Then of course there are other more personal reasons for discouragement. There are days when the increasing difficulties of life take toll of native buoyancy and resilience, moods when the daily drudgery does not seem to add up to a meaningful existence, hours when the realization begins to dawn that time is growing short and many of the things once dreamed and planned will never now be done, days when the mists close in and the fog comes down. Some years ago in London there was a dreadful December fog which lasted for days and nights on end, a literally killing fog; the death rate rose steeply. Just so, there can be spiritual fogs that choke the life of the spirit and kill faith. Who among us has never had to face something of this suffocating fog, this stifling feeling of depression?

Today let us approach this matter by way of an immensely moving page of Old Testament biography. It is the story of a man of like passions with ourselves. Here was David, at the very lowest and most atrociously discouraging point of his strange checkered career. If ever a man had legitimate cause for feeling depressed, David had at this juncture of his life.

Consider the situation. For years before this he had been the victim of the crazed, fanatical fury of King Saul. Saul's spear was at his throat. Eventually he had saved his life only by fleeing and casting himself on the not so tender mercies of his former foes the Philistines. Things surely had come to a pretty pass when David had to go seeking sanctuary from the Philistines, of all people. They had welcomed him with sardonic glee, gloating over this strange reversal of fate. They had given him, as a place of refuge, the town of Ziklag, away down in the south country, and in return David, with his little band of desperate men, volunteered to serve as a guerrilla detachment in the Philistine wars.

But further troubles were brewing. Some of the Philistines, perhaps not unreasonably, began to grow suspicious of their new ally. They were not sure of David and his men. They eyed them doubtfully. "What are those Hebrews doing here?" they asked. "How are we to know that they are not up to some subtle treachery?" The upshot was that David and his men were disarmed and demobilized and ordered back to their billets in Ziklag, there to be interned. But worse was to follow. For when they returned to Ziklag, they found to their dismay that in their absence the place had been raided by the Amalekites from over the border, their temporary homes destroyed, their buildings razed to the ground, their womenfolk carried off captive, nothing left but a heap of smoking ruins.

There was still worse to come. The last drop was now to be added to David's cup of sorrows. His own men mutinied. His best and most loyal followers turned against him. This last misfortune—the burning of their homes, the loss of their wives— was more than they could bear. Their morale collapsed. Their rage focused itself upon their leader. They cursed David to his face. They spoke of stoning him. He stood there friendless and forsaken.

Surely if ever a man had reason for wallowing in a veritable pit of dejection, David had then. He might easily have let himself go in a diatribe of scathing invective, impeaching the government of the universe. "Providence? What has providence done for me since the day when it sent Samuel to delude and fool me with the mad dream that I was a man born to be king?" Humanly speaking, that should have been the way of it. How wonderful, then, to read—immediately following the devastating catalog of calamities—the quiet, moving words "David encouraged himself in the Lord his God"! There was no one else to do it. There was not one voice to rally the heroic element buried deep beneath the piled-up debris of disenchantment, not one friend to cry "Courage, brother! do not stumble, though the path be dark as night." As far as external encouragement was concerned, he was derelict and forlorn. Whereupon "he encouraged himself."

Are we perhaps too dependent on other people in our dejected hours? It is true, of course, that we are intended to lean our weakness on others' strength. This is one of the great functions of the Christian fellowship. The mutual sharing of a caring community is one of the essential marks of the church. Just as we are meant to help those in trouble and distress, so also we are permitted to supplement our own deficiencies by drawing on the resources and sympathy and support of others. But there is a point where God himself may have to say to us, "Son of man, stand upon your feet! Do not go always draining the virtue out of other people. Do not drip your depression on to other lives. See if you cannot discover, by the grace of heaven, some inward ultimate resource. Soldier of the cross, arise!"

"David encouraged himself." What is vital for us is to notice how he set about it. Observe first how he did not do it.

For one thing, he did not do it by wishful thinking. He did not try to climb out of his depression by practicing some comfortable self-deception on his soul. Do we not take that way sometimes? The technique of the wishful thinker is this: if there are dark, disturbing facts, pretend they are not there. If there are grim disquieting realities, look the other way, and banish them from thought. Tell your soul, "Easy now! Go easy. Everything is bound to come out all right at last." This is the way of the wishful thinker. And this is how a good many seek to encourage themselves in the day of depression. I do not need to argue against it here. It bears its condemnation on its face; for obviously it is tampering with truth. There can be no honorable victory that way.

Notice, further, that if David did not encourage himself by wishful thinking, neither did he do it by stoic resolution. He did not seek to win through by lecturing his own soul on the matter of morale.

This indeed is a much nobler way than the other. The technique of the stoic is: Soul of mine, play the man! If things are grim, bear them grimly. If facts are stern, face them with a will of steel. Prove to all the world that, come what may, you are master of your fate and captain of your soul. When you are nearing the end of your tether, remember it is always possible to hold on a little longer. Ask not for any supernatural aids. Take your salvation into your own hands. Summon up the latent fortitude of your own soul. Resist the devil of depression, and he will flee from you!

That is the way of the stoic. This is how many fine spirits have encouraged themselves in the day of dejection. No one will question its nobility. It has been preached with passion all the way from Marcus Aurelius to Emily Brontë. But suppose that today I could tell you of no better way than that, suppose the church had no deeper answer to the human malady and predicament, how poverty-stricken the message, how woefully inadequate!

No, it was not by any arid stoicism that David sought to encourage himself, not by wishful thinking, not by saying "Now, David, it is always possible to endure a little longer; you don't know what unexpected change of fortune may be waiting for you round the next corner of the road." All that platitudinous humanist wisdom which boggles at the supernatural has not the first beginnings of the glimmering of a gospel. "David encouraged himself in the Lord his God."

This is the saving attitude, the real differentia of the man of faith. This is why the church has a word to communicate to this generation quite different from any word that politics can speak, or the press or the scientific humanist or the consulting room of the psychologist.

He encouraged himself in the Lord his God. I can imagine how David did it. He looked back to the happy days when God had spoken to the shepherd lad beside the sheepfold on the Bethlehem hills. He remembered how he had sung then of the goodness and mercy that shone in the sunshine across the green pastures and suffused even the dark eerie valleys of danger. Was that supernatural light gone for ever? Saul had outlawed him. The Philistines had disowned him. The Amalekites had robbed him. His own men had all but stoned him. But one thing neither Saul nor the Philistines, not the Amalekites nor his own men could ever do; they could not prevent him from letting God in upon his situation!

You can almost hear him doing it. "The Lord doth reign! Not Saul yonder on the throne of Israel. Not the princes of Philistia in their cities by the sea. Not the captains and the kings of Amalek. God on the throne of earth and heaven! This Lord is my shepherd still: I shall not want. Perish the low faithless mood. Get behind me, Satan." David was not going to let the devil in his desperate situation blind him to the one factor that supremely mattered. "I shall not die, but live, and declare the works of the Lord!"

This is the higher realism. But today you have this extraordinary ironical situation—so many people claiming precisely to be realists, scientific realists, claiming to be mature, adult personalities, fully come of age—because in assessing a total situation they are resolved not to admit the existence of any factors outside human categories, any elements of the transcendent and supernatural. There are even certain new theologies whose newness consists in playing down this element in the biblical picture, eliminating the factors of transcendence and supernaturalism, thinking to appeal to modern man by talking no longer, as the Bible does, of God the sovereign Creator, over against me, succoring, demanding, invading, helping—theologies which would have me find the ground of my being and the source of my salvation simply in my inner psychology and ultimate concern. Of that attitude it ought to be said that not only is it thoroughly mistaken, it is philosophically unsound. It is the very bankruptcy of realism. It is ignoring a whole sector of human experience. In the forthright words of a distinguished scientist and Christian believer, Professor C. A. Coulson, "A denial of God is practically always the result of shutting one eye. It may be for this reason that God gave us two."

Here in David's story is the higher realism in action. Over against his crushing calamities he set this: Saul and the Philistines and the Amalekites had stolen his home, his rights, his liberties; had they stolen his God? A thousand times, no! "They lost everything they had," exclaims Augustine, describing what happened to the Christians of the Empire when the barbarian hordes came down like a great surging flood that crashed through the barricades of civilization—"They lost everything they had; did they lose their faith?" And Augustine's great successor of a thousand years later, Martin Luther, sent the same trumpet note ringing round Europe, "And were this world all devils o'er and watching to devour us"—what matter?—"the city of God remaineth!"

This is the characteristic attitude of the man of faith in every age—not stoicism, not fantasy nor credulity, not muddle-headed, pious rhetoric that builds its house of life precariously on the sands of sentiment, but solid, basic realism, with its roots right down to the everlasting rock—"I believe in God the Father Almighty." Time and again as a minister of the gospel I have been privileged to see men and women with that kind of faith. And then I have seen them with the rain descending and the floods coming and the winds blowing and beating upon their house of life, and it fell not, for it was founded on the rock.

Men and women, could we not be of that number? Let us believe our own faith. In the day of dejection, do not shy off from the supernatural. Do not slam the door on the God who made you, and without whom you are going to be restless for ever. Remember your life has all round it at this moment, at every moment, the dimension of the transcendent and the eternal. Encourage yourself in the Lord your God!

You and I have a far stronger motive for doing this than even David had. He had not seen Christ—we have. In Christ we have seen, as he never did, the veil that shrouds the mystery of human existence rent in twain from the top to the bottom, and the very heart of God made plain. Can we distrust a love that blazed out in the flame of Calvary? Can we disbelieve the power that turned that tragic hour to triumph? Can we forget how at one point after another of the road we have traveled the everlasting mercy has come to meet us—all the way back beyond our earliest memories to our very birth and baptism? What was that baptism of yours but God in Christ promising to be with you even to the end of the world? Luther, at one dark period of his life, was being tempted by the devil of discouragement, but when he had nothing else to hang on to, one phrase of two words he kept repeating as his last defiance, "Baptizatus sum," I have been baptized—as though to say, "Nothing can alter that! God will never be less loving than when in baptism Christ's name was sealed upon me." And in David's earlier life there had been that great day when he went out against Goliath. The Lord who delivered me from the lion and the bear," he had cried, "shall he not deliver me out of the hand of this Philistine?" He who delivered then, shall he not deliver now? "So long thy power hath blessed me," sang John Henry Newman, with the same logic of faith moving from past experience to future hope, "sure it still will lead me on." For Christ is the same yesterday, today, and for ever. Surely if David could encourage himself in the Lord his God, how much more we—who have seen the mightiest of all God's mighty acts, we who are heirs of the cross, sons and daughters of the resurrection! O loving God in Christ, your yoke is easy, and your burden light!

One thing remains to be added—and it comes at us straight out of this story of David. No man has a right to encourage himself in the Lord—unless he is prepared forthwith to act on the basis of that encouragement, and to act strenuously, radically and decisively.

The whole essence of faith is that we should proceed upon it, that we step out and act upon it. Look at David. If I were to think that encouraging himself in the Lord meant, for David, writing a few more consolatory psalms, saying a few more prayers, recalling a few more past experiences, it would simply show that I did not know David nor David's God. For see! In the very next verse after the word about encouragement, you find David girding on his harness, saying in effect what Saul of Tarsus was to say when he encountered Christ, "Lord, what wilt thou have me to do?" "David inquired of the Lord, Shall I pursue after this troop? Shall I overtake them?" In other words, faith is not faith until it goes to work in my life. And there is no final reinforcement from the Lord for me unless I am prepared now to take the divine will as it may be revealed and follow it out in action. There was a Scottish Douglas who carried with him on his campaigns a casket with the heart of the dead Bruce. "Forward, gallant heart!" he cried on one occasion, flinging the casket into the midst of a desperate fight, "forward as thou wert wont! Douglas will follow thee or die." Faith means saying something like this to Christ. It is not dreaming up an ideal of faith that makes any man a Christian. It is not correct theologizing that ultimately wins for any of us the encouragement of God. It is catching step with Christ's triumphant march. "Forward, gallant heart! My soul will follow Thee or die." "Christians," says Bishop Lesslie Newbigin, "are meant to be a task force rather than a study group or a holy club." And Charles Wesley said the same thing long ago:

> Ready for all Thy perfect will,
> My acts of faith and love repeat,
> Till death Thy endless mercies seal,
> And make the sacrifice complete.

There is a rather wonderful ending to this story. Do you know what happened immediately following the incidents recorded here? Looking at this battered exile, this hunted fugitive without a friend, one might have been pardoned for supposing his fortunes were so low that vindication could not come in a dozen years. In fact, it was just three days after his return from pursuing Amalek that there came a messenger from Mount Gilboa, with the news that Saul had fallen in battle and that Israel was now left leaderless, looking for a king. Three days from the fearful pit and the miry clay to the scepter and the throne! It is almost as if it had been meant to stand as a parable of Good Friday and Easter. Three days from "My God, why hast thou forsaken me?" to the sunburst of the resurrection; three days from the sorrows of death and the pains of hell to the throne of heaven and the empire of the world.

Of course I am not saying that faith will necessarily induce for us a swift, dramatic change in outer circumstances. That is always possible, since God is alive and the day of miracles is still here. But it does not have to happen that way. What I do say is that, let what will be the aspect of outer events, you can have the inner victory now—all dark depression scattered by the dawn, and the radiance of the divine love breaking through the midnight of the soul. By the grace of God, this could happen for someone here now, someone who perhaps turned into this church today depressed, apprehensive, discouraged, and will now—by the loving kindness of God—go out rejoicing, confident, tranquil, and serene. This is the Lord's doing. Lay that hand in the hand of Christ today, and renew your covenant with him.

> And so through all the length of days
> Thy goodness faileth never;
> Good Shepherd, may I sing Thy praise
> Within Thy house for ever!

WHEN THE VISION FADES

*"Demas hath forsaken me, having loved this present world,
and is departed unto Thessalonica."*
2 TIMOTHY 4:10

There are just three references to Demas in the New Testament.
The first is in Paul's letter to the Colossians, where we have
this, "Luke, the beloved physician, and Demas, greet you."
Obviously he was a man of note in the church, to have his name
thus coupled with Luke's. The second reference is in the short
letter to Philemon, "There salute you Mark, Aristarchus, Demas,
Luke, my fellow laborers"—again a sentence which implies that
Demas had an honored place in the exciting movement which
carried the gospel sweeping through the cities of Asia and
Europe. And then, without any further explanation, comes the
third, the final reference, this cry of an apostle imprisoned for
the faith and nearing the journey's end, "Demas hath forsaken
me, having loved this present world." The rest is silence.

Let us fill in the gaps. We can think, for example, of what a
mighty missionary Demas must have been in his day. When
the enthusiasm of his first conversion to the Christian faith was
burning within him, how he rejoiced whenever Paul chose him
out for special duty in Thessalonica or Colosse or Rome! When
in crowded marketplace or oriental bazaar he preached Christ's
death and risen life, always there were conversions following.
And when the door was shut at night and Demas was at his
prayers, what prayers they were—all a great gratitude to God
and an eager passion for souls! We may be sure that in many a
city of the Empire there were church members who could tell
that it was to this man, under God, that they owed their souls,

men and women who would be found in the kingdom of heaven at last because Demas had crossed their path. "My fellow laborer," Paul calls him, with gratitude and pride.

So for some years it lasted. And then—a cloud came over the sky, a cloud no bigger than a man's hand. And Paul saw it. Paul, listening to Demas reporting on his work, knew that something was wrong. His friend and fellow laborer was not happy: the old zest had vanished, the joy and certainty and conviction were stifled and inhibited. And Paul wondered why. Was it perhaps intellectual doubt that was the trouble? Was Christ seeming something less than the final clue to life's enigmas after all? Or was it a premonition of persecution, the rumblings of the gathering storm that was going to sweep the church and sift the wheat from the chaff? Or was it that the old life, so much less morally astringent and demanding, was catching up with him, suggesting to him, "Perhaps I could serve my generation equally well in other ways, with Christ not indeed left out but given a subordinate and somewhat less than absolute place among my secular interests"? So Paul watched and grieved to see the sunlit morning fading into fog and grayness and sullen skies.

Whither is fled the visionary gleam?
Where is it now, the glory and the dream?

The final interview took place in Rome. You can picture Demas visiting Paul in his prison that day. "I have come," he says, gazing at the ground, for he cannot look his friend and leader in the face, "I have come to hand back my commission. I have come to say good-bye." "But surely, Demas," cries Paul, "you are not drawing out now? You cannot mean that this is the end? Take time, and think again!" "No," he replies, I have indeed thought, through the long night watches I have racked my soul with thinking, and I hate to hurt you, but I must be free." "But Demas, my fellow laborer, my son in the faith," cries Paul, "it is not your hurting me that matters—that is the least of it. You are hurting Christ! The cause of Christ is needing you, and will you turn your back on him? Does not the cross on which he died for love of you, Demas, cut off your contemplated retreat and hold you to the path of loyalty and honor?" "Yes, but Paul," retorts the other, "look how the cause has grown. Christ has his missionaries all over the world now. Surely he will never miss me. What difference can one more or less make? Anyway, it is settled; my mind is made up, and I am going. I leave Rome tonight!" "So be it, then," replies Paul. "But Demas, friend, remember this, after being with Christ, as you these past years have been with him, learning to walk in his light which is the very radiance of eternity, nothing on earth is ever going to satisfy you again." But Demas went. And Paul that night, his eyes dimmed with tears, took up his pen and wrote, "Demas hath forsaken me, having loved this present world."

Now that phrase raises a crucial question. What does "the love of the world" mean? In what does it consist? We have to go very carefully here, for there has been much confusion about this, even among Christian people.

Is it, for instance, true to say that it is a Christian's duty to hold aloof from the world, and thoroughly to segregate the sacred from the secular? When Robert Browning breaks out singing:

How good is man's life, the mere living! how fit to employ
All the heart and the soul and the senses, for ever in joy! —

is Christian piety, hearing that, to look slightly shocked? "How good the mere living! Employ the senses in joy—is that not pagan?" Are we to accept the view that Christian discipleship means a negation of secular involvement, means not getting caught up in the world and its concerns, but saving our immortal souls out of it? Is this what Scripture means when it condemns the love of the world?

So at any rate the church in certain moods and at certain times has seemed to think. But that is a calamitous misinterpretation of Christ.

Before we can see what this damaging love of the world is, we had better be clear what it is not. Do you remember who it was who said, "I am the spirit of negation"? That was Goethe's Mephistopheles. Jesus never said that or anything like it. On the contrary! Don't think, Paul begged the Corinthians, that Christ is a negation of the world or of our essential humanity, God's categorical no: Christ is the everlasting yea, God's world-affirming yes! "All the promises of God are yea and amen in him." In Christ, cries John, God so loved the world! And never for an instant is the world out of God's hands.

The best Christians in every age have understood this. When Pascal, one of the seventeenth century's mightiest intellects, was converted to Christ, something like a wave of exuberant irrepressible gaiety passed over him, so much so that his own sister Jacqueline remonstrated. "But my brother," she said, "what will your spiritual director think of such a gleeful penitent?" When Rabbi Duncan found the light, "I danced," said he, "on the old Brig O'Dee at Aberdeen for sheer delight!" And there was Francis too, that great lover of the world. "Who are you?" they asked him, as he and his companions went singing by. "We are the minstrels of Christ," he would answer, "troubadours of God!" That is the faith of Christ: not a world-despising thing shunning the secular as though it were somehow irrelevant or unclean; nor the pompous dreariness of church services which, lacking all notes of spontaneity and conviction and joy, serve only to widen the credibility gap, and to confirm the outsider in his determination to stay outside; but a thing all zest and gladness and sympathy and understanding and fellow-feeling, deeply involved in the world at every turn, rejoicing in the free flowering of the human spirit, and refusing to departmentalize experience into secular and sacred, that utterly false dichotomy, for the whole world is God's—and God so loved the world.

Do you remember that when Jesus died on Calvary they nailed above his head a title written in three languages? "This is Jesus the King"—in Latin, Greek, and Hebrew. There is a startling symbolism in that. Hebrew was the sacred language, but Latin and Greek were secular—Latin the language of politics and government, Greek the language of art and culture. Why was it not written up only in Hebrew? That would have made sense, if Jesus (as some would have us believe) has only an incidental concern with politica and culture. But look at it! "This is Jesus the King," in Greek—the language of Homer and Aeschylus, Plato and Pheidias, and all the culture of that ancient world. "This is Jesus the King," in Latin—the language of Caesar and Cicero and Livy and all the politicians of the day. Yes, Pilate, you were right! For they are all Christ's, culture and politics, commerce and society. He is the desire of nations. All life is his. And therefore it is ours, if we are his—in whom God so loved the world.

You can take it a stage further and say that all the men and women in the world are Christ's. People with whom some Christians would rather not mix because they seem totally alien and irreligious, the angry young men and the rebels, the intellectuals and the skeptics and the agnostics, the drug addicts and the alcoholics—they, too, are Christ's. They, too, have been made in the image of God, rooted in the divine creativity, their very existence grounded (though they may not know it) in the will of God. If we despise them, we are despising Christ. If we stand aloof from them, we stand aloof from Christ. If we patronize them, well, does not the Bible say "Inasmuch as ye did it to one of the least of these, ye did it unto me"? We are patronizing Christ. Do not let us in a sanctified individualism narrow down the world-encompassing religion of Jesus. It has room for every sphere of existence, a sense of solidarity with all creation, and love for all mankind. God so loved the world!

What, then, is this love of the world which wrecked Demas and can wreck us still? We have seen what it is not. What is it? It is anything in life that crowds Christ out. It is things that may in themselves be perfectly innocuous, twining and twisting themselves about my soul, until I cannot reach up any longer to God my judge and my redeemer. It is anything that makes me forget, or even temporarily want to forget, that my citizenship is in heaven. It is anything that eliminates from my horizon the dimension of eternity. That is what the Word of God is condemning.

You may have met a man who tells you quite frankly that his great ambition in life is to make money. He may be an honorable man; he may indeed be doing a power of good. But that affluent life-style is his chief ambition. That is the love of the world. You have seen people conforming to convention till they were just fashion-ridden by the standards of a social set, their dominant passion being to keep up with their neighbors and to rise in the social scale, and not in the least perturbed by the fact that 20 percent of the earth's population consume 80 percent of the earth's resources. That is the love of the world. I have heard of a family where a son, a brilliant student, felt moved to offer himself for missionary service, and the family said, "Drop it! Be sensible. Stay where you are!" That family was the entrenched principle of the love of the world.

There is a parable of our Lord's about a man who made a big success of life. He was completely absorbed in his fields and barns and stackyards—and mark you, he was right to be absorbed in them: it was his duty. But this man was so absorbed that eventually it had the effect of quite desupernaturalizing his life. And what shall it profit a man to gain the whole world, and lose his own soul? Here was Demas, who had been with Paul in Rome and with Christ at a hundred communion tables. Here he was back in Thessalonica, trying to find an authentic existence for himself by mitigating Christ's totalitarian demands, as though the fellowship of his sufferings and the power of his resurrection did not matter vitally after all. "Having loved the present world."

I wonder if this Demas malady ever infects the church? Would it not have to be said that if a church begins to measure its achievements, pointing to big numbers, bustling organizations, thriving finance as a success story justifying its activities; if it is concerned about status symbols, press opinions, the patronage of influential people; if chameleonlike it adapts its color to whatever may be the dominant contemporary philosophy or popular trend, producing a new theology, a new morality, a new situation ethic to suit the requirements of the current mood, or even if its rightful concern for social justice in this world becomes so absorbing that it scarce has anything to say about the life of the world to come; or if its no less rightful reaction against a false individualism is causing it to soft-pedal the note of personal religion, till it almost ceases to speak about individual salvation at all—would it not have to be said that this is just Demas all over again?

Bring it right down to ourselves. We have all felt the magnetism of Christ, the bracing challenge of his "Follow me," the haunting sense that if the meaning of existence is to be found anywhere it is to be found in him. And yet—are there no rivals to his allegiance, no "dearest idols I have known," no prudential considerations or respectable rational arguments drawing me the other way? Each of us in his own heart knows all too well the answer to that question. This is the love of the world—anything, good, bad, or indifferent that disinclines me for Jesus, any compromise that crowds out God.

So Demas went. But suppose we could carry the story further. Suppose we could see him away yonder in Thessalonica with the Christian adventure all behind him now, and with the strain relaxed and the tension finished. Do you think he was happy and at peace?

Outwardly, no doubt, everything in Thessalonica was the same as he had known it in the old pre-Christian days, just the same as ever. And yet—the same? I think not. For Christ had come in between, Christ the disturber and tormentor, Christ of the far horizons and the splendid dreams, Christ the reality behind all fantasies. There is a poem by Mary Webb which tells of a human love that came, and then was lost. Imagine this addressed, not to a human beloved, but to Christ:

> Why did you come, with your enkindled eyes
> And mountain-look, across my lower way,
> And take the vague dishonour from my day
> By luring me from paltry things, to rise
> And stand beside you, waiting wistfully
> The looming of a larger destiny?

Why did you with strong fingers fling aside
The gates of possibility, and say
With vital voice the words I dream to-day?
Before, I was not much unsatisfied:
But since a god has touched me and departed,
I run through every temple, broken-hearted.

There was Demas, back in Thessalonica, "having loved this present world." There were voices in the wind that seemed to cry aloud, "Demas, you fool! Disciple Demas, who felt the refiner's fire of the joy of Christ, luring you away from paltry things to rise and stand beside him, did you think you could now be satisfied with the narrow horizon and the dull distasteful tedium of an unredeemed existence? Run through every temple, broken-hearted, and the very stones will cry out, 'Demas, you fool!' "

But no, Demas, I cannot call you that. For doubtless, Demas, you were cradled in a loving mother's arms, and her prayers for you would never cease. And Demas, there is that house church which once meant so much to you—your former companions there are feeling sad and bereft without you. And you say, Demas, you cannot help it; it is how you are made, and these others do not understand; and you are glad to be rid of the large destiny and the haunting dream and the preposterous demand. Oh Demas, foolish, beloved Demas, how Christ has spoiled you for anything else for ever!

And so for us. One vision of what life with Christ can mean, one taste of that ampler, far more meaningful existence that is his gift, and we are never going to be content with the narrowness of an earthbound experience, with hopes unrealized and dissolving dreams. And when the love of the world beckons, we had best remember that.

And remember also this. The only way ultimately to defeat the love of the world, to control a natural passion, is not to repress it, but to set against it a supernatural passion. This is what the church ought to be doing for the thousands of unanchored and alienated folk today, who are restlessly running from one experiment to the next in the quest for true significance and an authentic existence. What they are really needing—though they do not know it—is something deeper than all their experimenting to achieve self-identity. It is something to worship: it is the supernatural, the magnificence of Christ and the majesty of God. And so often, alas! the church has tried to win them the wrong way, has tried to attract them by its broad humanity, by its likeness to themselves, by the undemanding lowness of its creed, its almost apologetic tone for having a creed at all. They don't want that: they can get that in a club, and get it better. Certainly our young intelligent agnostics don't want that. They want a divine supernatural presence. They want the life of God. They want the sacramental realism of Christ.

This is what thousands of spiritually hungry souls are needing at this moment for the realization of their hopes. When a Roman recruit joined his legion, "I swear," he would say, lifting up his hand to heaven and taking the vow which was his "sacramentum," "I swear to follow the eagles of Caesar wherever they fly." And he knew what it meant—follow them up to Hadrian's Wall and Caledonia or down to the Ganges and the Nile, over the cold snows of Germany or the blazing sands of Africa—"I follow the eagles of Caesar!"—his sacramentum. And we have a sacrament too, in Holy Communion, yes, but also in the common life of every day—the abiding presence, the far vision and the ratified vow: "I follow Christ my king, through light and dark, through life and death—I follow the King!"

I sometimes wonder if Demas came back. I almost believe he did. You see, if Demas wanted to be left undisturbed and at peace in his world, he should not have gone to Thessalonica. Not there! For Thessalonica was the home of a great Christian church. I see him going along a street in Thessalonica one day, and he hears from a building nearby the sound of singing. It is a psalm of David, "How lovely are thy tabernacles, O Lord of hosts, my King of my God! Blessed are they who dwell in thy house: they will be still praising thee." And Demas stops, as if struck. "How lovely are thy dwellings!—and I have no place there now. I have thrown away the title-deeds of my inheritance.

Should I go back?" And the psalm is followed by a Christian hymn, "Awake, thou that sleepest, and arise from the dead, and Christ shall give thee light." He did it once for you, Demas; will he again? "Should I go back? I must go back. I must get home again!"

Did he? I cannot tell. I should love to think he did. I should love to think of Paul writing another letter and including this— "Demas has returned to me, having loved Christ far better than anything else in the world: he has returned, and will stay this time for ever!"

Perhaps he did. I don't know. But I do know this: anyone can. It is not a long journey, like the road from Thessalonica to Rome. It is a single step. Even "the far country" Jesus spoke of is only a single step from the Father's home. One word, one prayer, one verse of a hymn perhaps—and you are there. It could happen even in that verse of Isaac Watts's greatest hymn we are about to sing:

Were the whole realm of Nature mine,
   That were an offering far too small;
Love so amazing, so divine,
   Demands my soul, my life, my all.

A single step! Such is the overflowing mercy of God, the love that passes knowledge. Surely and indeed, love so amazing demands my life today.

THE POWER TO HEAL

" 'If You can do anything, have pity on us and help us.'
And Jesus said to him, 'If You can!
All things are possible to him who believes.'
Immediately the father of the child cried out and said,
'I believe; help my unbelief!' . . .
And when He had entered the house,
His disciple asked Him privately, 'Why could we not cast it out?' "
MARK 9:22,23,24,28 (RSV)

When Raphael set himself to represent the Transfiguration, he painted two pictures in one. He depicted, on the mountaintop, the glorified Lord, luminous and radiant in the splendor of heaven. But down beneath, he also portrayed on the same canvas the pitiful spectacle of the demon-possessed lad and his distracted father and the crowd surging around. Two separate pictures in one. It is as though Raphael by his art were trying to demonstrate how inextricably they belong together—the desperate human situation down here on earth, and the grace and glory of the eternal; the gaping need of this demented and delirious world and the healing power of the unseen. They belong together, and what God has joined together let not man put asunder.

But the disquieting thing is that so often we seem to be doing our best to put them asunder. There are two opposite mistakes we make.

One is Peter's mistake. You might call this the mistake of the other-worldly. "Master," said Peter on the Transfiguration mountain, "let us stay up here. We will build here three tabernacles, one for you, one for Moses, one for Elijah." It is as if he were saying, "Let us forget that turbulent, distracted world below, all the fever and the fret down there where men toil and struggle and complain and sin. Why break our hearts on the stony recalcitrance of Galilee or the political hostility of Jerusalem, when there is this mystic communion so richly to enjoy? Let us perpetuate the beatific vision and bask on the sunny shores of the eternal!"

It is a real temptation for some professing Christians still. Talk to them about the world's plight in this revolutionary age, or even about the tragic misunderstanding between the church and masses of people in an industrial society, and it simply induces in them a feeling of helplessness in face of secularism's massive menace. "In any case," they may explain, "we are not clear that all that is our business." So they withdraw into their religious shell, cultivating a personal devotional life and letting the world go careering on its headstrong way. Sometimes the church itself has been tempted to take that path of withdrawal, disowning its redemptive mission to the world, refusing to become involved with a secular society, and thereby ceasing to be Messianic. It is then we need to hear such a word as Jesus must have spoken to Peter: "Come back to earth, man! Here is this clamorous human situation. Come right back into it." And if we should hesitate, on he goes alone, striding down the hill without us to where the need is greatest, for he cannot stay out of it.

Is this not the inner meaning of the incarnation itself? What was that event but just God coming right down into the tumult and the shouting of the world? In the most literal sense, it was a down-to-earth realism that gave the gospel birth, and we Christians can stay out of the tension and the tumult only at the price of being disloyal to our Lord.

But perhaps it is the other mistake, the opposite mistake, into which most of us are liable to fall: not the mistake of Peter and James and John up there on the slopes of Hermon, but the mistake of the other nine disciples down at the foot of the mountain. If the former was the mistake of the other-worldly, here we have the mistake of the this-worldly. For there were those nine disciples, confronting the tragic situation focused in this demented creature, and thinking to resolve it out of their own personal resources, with no aid of power from the beyond. Christ seemed to be lost. His presence had been withdrawn. This is precisely how the church has felt in times of the ebbing of the tide of faith, when the winds of revival have ceased to blow. Christ, as those disciples figured it, was somewhere up among the clouds. There was no saying when his presence would be restored to them. But what matter, when there was such an obvious task in front of them? Were they not practical men, with skill, initiative, ingenuity? They would tackle this crisis without difficulty. They would heal the sufferer's misery. They would exorcise the devil successfully!

This is the other blunder, the opposite blunder to Peter's: to go out to deal with the tangled human situation—yes, and with the crisis of the church—with all kinds of man-made schemes and remedies, but not with God's glory, God's mighty act of redeeming grace, dominating all our thoughts. "Wait on the Lord?" men say. "Work and pray for conversions? Oh, do be practical! We cannot dally for a Christ who is lost up yonder in the clouds. We need not try to meet a revolutionary situation with a religious idealism. This is no time to be talking of the new birth, or spiritual commitment, or the life of prayer. Face the hard logic of facts. Mankind has to set its own house in order, and redeem itself now or within these next few years from the overhanging threat of doom and destruction. What then? Given goodwill and cooperation, intelligence and rational planning, surely it can redeem itself effectively enough!"

So men say. So sometimes even the church has seemed to say. And still, amid the shouts and tumult in the valley, the plight of the patient is unrelieved. Still this poor lad at the foot of the mountain was torn and tortured with his demons. Still the desperate predicament of humanity remains unresolved.

At this point we must come more closely to grips with the tense drama of the story. Picture the tumultuous scene that met Christ's view on his descent from the mountain: in the very center of the crowd his own disciples, with the scribes and Pharisees quizzing and cross-questioning them, pelting them with taunts they could not answer, so that they were feeling crushed and cowed and baffled, and round about, a great throng of people, taking sides in the debate, bandying advice and shouting comments, a terrific din and wrangle—the same kind of loud frenetic clamor that fills the world and rings in our ears today.

What was it all about, this debate? Mainly, no doubt, it was a question of diagnosis. It was a dispute about modes of treatment. Here was this poor distracted creature—and remember we are taking him as typifying the whole predicament of humanity today. Here was the suffering patient, and here were the disputers with their advice. You can almost hear them at it. They are at it still today.

Thus some, I have no doubt, would be saying—as in fact they are saying now—"It is all a matter of education. If this unfortunate sufferer had had a rational upbringing, he would never have landed in this plight. Even yet, if you give him the appropriate educative treatment, it may be you will heal him of his frenzy and turn him into a useful member of society again."

Others again, I imagine, would have a different diagnosis. "It is the home background that has been wrong, the actual physical environment that has been defective. You must house him properly. Get him out to the suburbs, to one of the new desirable building estates. Make his surroundings right, and that will be the first step to making his soul right."

Still others would have a different remedy. They would look at this poor creature and say—"It is all the fault of the social system. We want a rationalized way of living, a planned economy. Then perhaps these tragedies will disappear."

Education, housing, social betterment—yes indeed, we need all this. And with no uncertain voice the Christian conscience ought to be demanding it. Here Christian action must not bring up the rear, but be out in front, giving a lead. But by themselves, and even taken all together, they are still not adequate. You can confer all manner of benefits on men, and yet leave their souls a shambles of meaninglessness, discontent, and disenchantment.

So it was that here at the foot of the hill the dispute went on, some suggesting one thing, some another, and in the heat of it, the poor demon-ridden sufferer himself was almost quite forgotten.

Then Jesus came. Now note this significant touch the evangelist has included. "Immediately all the crowd, when they saw him, ran up to him and greeted him."

I am not surprised that those badgered disciples ran to him. That indeed is understandable. "Here is Jesus at last—thank heaven for that!" You see, this debate had worried them, all the quizzing and badgering they had been subjected to had frightened them. The mocking, skeptical faces round them seemed to say, "You may as well give it up, and confess you are beaten. All your grand claims to deal with the powers of darkness and to exorcise the demons were nonsense after all!" They had felt so feeble and futile in the Master's absence. Somehow, when he was not there, the prevailing atmosphere of skepticism and unbelief seemed to infiltrate their minds and suffocate their faith.

You cannot inhale a skeptical atmosphere without the danger of being infected. The church knows that. There have been periods when the Christian church has lost touch with its own Lord, and then the skepticism of the secular society around has gotten under its defenses, laying a withering blight upon the church itself.

But here, suddenly, "Look, Matthew," cried Thomas, "look, Philip and Nathanael, see where he comes again!" And with an immense relief surging in their hearts, they went running to him.

And the church knows that experience too: after the dead periods and the eclipse of faith, the sudden vision and the spirit of renewal. "O Christ, you have come back to us—thank heaven!" And Christian men have thrown off the infection and poison of unbelief that had weakened and unnerved them, and stood their ground with the skeptics. "They say. What say they? Let them say!"

But you will notice it was not only the disciples who went running to Jesus; it was "all the people," the whole multitude. That surely is significant. The crowd had looked with amused derision on the helplessness of Christ's followers. How could they do otherwise after such a lamentable failure? But here was the Man himself. This was different. Something might really happen now!

Today the world may well be disillusioned in us who are Christ's followers. But the real hope of the situation is that the world is not yet disillusioned in Christ. Time and again we have failed him and misrepresented him and have dimmed the light most lamentably; but dimly and afar, the light still shines. And when you have painted your somber picture of humanity today, with its moral collapse, its drift from religion, and its discord and frustration, you must set this down also if you want your picture to be true—the magnetism of the untarnished shining character of Jesus, towering above the wrecks of time, and the ineluctable feelings in a myriad hearts that if anyone has the answer to mankind's precarious situation it is this Man who has it. "Is there any word from the Lord?"

Such a word indeed there is. It is here in the story. "Bring him to me!" This is the cry that rang out above the chaos here when Christ stepped in and took control. "Where is this unhappy sufferer? Bring him to me."

With that absolute consciousness of adequate resources Christ confronts the human dilemma today. Others have tried to heal the world's hurt—humanists, philosophers, system-makers—and still the desperate plight remains, "Bring it to me!" The church has tried and failed too often, and the world has gone away disappointed, "Bring it to me!" And it could be that now Christ is speaking personally and individually to someone here, saying, "My friend, there is that unsolved problem in your life, that haunting doubt, that tangled situation, that old wound still unhealed: bring it to me!"

"I found," said Augustine, "in my studies of Plato and Cicero many fine things acutely said, but in none of them did I find 'Come unto me, and rest.' " No, indeed. For that is Christ alone.

KING FOR EVER

120

And it is with that same amazing consciousness of power today that he confronts the unhealed hurt of humanity. "Bring it to me!"

So the father brought his poor demented child. "If you can do anything, have pity on us and help us." Notice that poignant plural—"Have pity on us." Not only on him, the suffering child—"have pity on us." This is the solidarity of sorrow. It is unfortunate that at this point the familiar words of the Authorized Version have obscured the real force of Christ's reply as it stands in the original, but the Revised Standard Version has restored it. What actually happened was this. Jesus, quick as lightning, fixed on the implied question mark in the man's mind: "If you can? Is that your doubt? Whether I really possess the power to do this thing? No, you have the 'If' in the wrong place. There is indeed an 'If' in this matter, but it is not where you are putting it. If I can—is that the trouble? If I possess the power? No, friend, if you can—that is the crux of it. If you can believe, all things are possible!"

And here are we today, looking out on this chaos of a world —perhaps also on the church, with its elaborate structure and competent machinery too often dull and lusterless—and then looking up to God in heaven and crying rather tentatively, "If thou, Lord, canst do anything about it!" Back sounds the answer, with a thousand trumpets in it, "If thou canst? That— to God? No! If you can believe! If you, doubting church, problem-haunted world, earthbound soul, if you can rise to faith!" That is the only "If" in the matter. The other side is certain. All things are possible to him who believes.

"Lord, I believe," said this man, "help my unbelief!" And there he speaks for all. For life so often is not all belief or unbelief, but a strange baffling mixture of both. These are the perplexing relativities of our religion. Robert Browning's vivid description is familiar:

> With me, faith means perpetual unbelief
> Kept quiet like the snake 'neath Michael's foot
> Who stands calm just because he feels it writhe.

THE POWER TO HEAL

121

But what precisely did this man mean when he cried "I do believe, but help my unbelief"? Was it "Help my unbelief to grow into faith"? Or was it "Help me in any case, unbelieving though I be"? I think the latter. "Don't let my faith or lack of it decide. Let your grace alone decide." And there he speaks for all.

And because God delights in mercy, here in the story the prayer was answered—the tearing, foaming demon cast out, and the sufferer's long misery healed. Then at the end comes that lovely touch, "Jesus took him by the hand, and lifted him up."

When it was all over, the disciples brought their question, "Why could we not cast it out?" "We had our chance and were not able to take it. We have been just as futile as all the rest. We, your followers, Jesus, ought surely to have been adequate to the situation. Tell us why we were not!" And that question finds an echo across the years, Why cannot the church do it? To all of which Christ's answer is very frank and searching. "This kind goes not forth—there is no means of driving out this type of evil—but by prayer and fasting."

The word "fasting" is absent from a number of the earliest Greek manuscripts, and some commentators have queried its position here, suggesting it may have been added by a later scribe. But in any case it stands for a deep truth spoken of elsewhere by Jesus quite explicitly. For what the word connotes is self-discipline, hard training, a kind of spiritual athleticism in discipleship—very different from the slack and flabby attitude of compromising, halfhearted mediocrity into which it is so easy to fall. It means a quality of life alert and dynamic and flexible in the hands of God.

Who of us does not realize the danger of thinking that we can serve the Lord without the cost of a radical consecration? There was a characteristic remark of Dr. Alexander Whyte to a young man who had come through a sudden spiritual experience and was confident that everything in the Christian life was going to be easy ever afterwards. The old man shook his head.

"My son," he said, "it is going to be a sore warstle to the end of the road!" When they were excavating the great Roman Wall across the north from the Solway to the Tyne, they came upon a monument reared by legionaries in that dim and distant past, and there with astonished eyes they read the inscription: "In disciplinam Augustorum" to the discipline of the emperors. On a different level, it is something not unlike that which the New Testament means by fasting. For the Christian must be a spiritual athlete, disciplined by a divine Commander, glorifying God in his body and in his spirit, which are God's.

And the other thing is prayer. "This kind of evil can be mastered only by prayer." Prayer is indeed a tremendous activity. For it means letting the divine in upon a human situation, supplying the condition in which the living God gets a purchase upon events, lifting up the conflict and the chaos into direct contact with the energy and power of the supernatural. By prayer, men have shaken nations. By prayer, they have cast out demons. By prayer, dead hopes have become resurgent and victorious. By prayer, the church of dry bones in Ezekiel's vision became a mighty marching army. Why, then, should we Christians—after all the great things God has done for us in the past, and all we have experienced of the power of Christ—why be content with a slack conventional discipleship, when through the prayer of faith we might be preparing a way for the Lord, and making straight through the desert of these days a highway for our God?

Lord, increase our faith! Lord, when we are feeling feeble and feckless and at the end of our tether, drive it home to us that firm as a rock stands the ancient promise of power from on high, and that the offer of resources from away beyond this present world is valid for ever and authentic here and now! Lord, we believe; help thou our unbelief. And to Christ's dear name be the glory.

CHRIST AT THE DOOR

*"Behold, I stand at the door, and knock:
if any man hear My voice, and open the door, I will come in to him,
and will sup with him, and he with Me."*
REVELATION 3:20

Beethoven's fifth symphony, the great C minor, is built up around a single phrase of music, now known throughout the world. It is a sequence of four notes only—one short note three times repeated, followed immediately by a longer note lower down the scale—and this dominating phrase, appearing and reappearing from the first bar of the symphony to the last, helps to give the music its rugged rhythm and momentum. During the Second World War, it was this phrase which became the secret V sign for conquered Europe. Tradition has not been slow to tell us what that haunting four-note sequence represents. "Thus fate knocks at the door" is said to have been Beethoven's own account of it. Whether that interpretation really tallies with the composer's inmost mind is perhaps doubtful. But certain it is that those sudden dramatic opening notes, repeated and re-echoed all the way through, do convey with extraordinary vividness an imperious rap, tap at a closed gate, an inexorable, peremptory summons to draw back the bolts and stand and deliver.

"Thus fate knocks at the door." But what is fate? Some there are who, looking out upon the mystery of this strange life where we seem driven this way and that by forces beyond our control, speak of fate, others call it God. Where the fatalist can hear only the remorseless rhythm of the march of history, pounding out its ominous refrain, the Christian hears the living

voice of the eternal. *"Behold, I stand at the door, and knock."*
Apply this to the present time. Above the tumult and the
shouting of contemporary history with all its hectic rivalry of
contradictory ideologies, and through the deafening clamor and
chaos of this confused, bewildered age, there comes—if you
will hear it—a deeper sound, clear, penetrating, unmistakable—
not fate, but God, knocking at the door.

I sometimes wonder if we Christians are alert enough to
hear it. It is perhaps significant that the word used in the original
Greek does not mean a gentle tap: it is the word for knocking
with a staff. Walter de la Mare has a poem describing a horse-
man knocking at the door of a lonely house in the depths of
the forest, with no response from the phantom listeners within.

> For he suddenly smote on the door, even
> Louder, and lifted his head: —
> "Tell them I came, and no one answered,
> That I kept my word," he said.

And indeed in our generation God has kept his word. There
has been through these years a sound—not the hand of fate,
but the hand of God, knocking at the door.

For consider this. Here is this twentieth century civilization
trying hurriedly to readjust its ways of life to the startling,
incredible leap forward of scientific knowledge; this generation
which has seen so many romantic illusions of human brotherhood and peace go whistling down the wind, and so much
utopian optimism shattered into fragments; this world that is
beginning to realize it may be easier to send an astronaut to the
moon than to rescue an alcoholic or a drug addict, easier and
possibly less important to fling men into space than to teach
them to walk with dignity and humility on earth. Here is this
world that is beginning at last to sense the disquieting truth
(which indeed Jesus and the gospel have always proclaimed)
that man left to himself is fundamentally incapable of resolving
the problem of his destiny. Left to himself he will never make
this earth a paradise of peace, fraternity, and security. And what
is all that discovery—that bad news about man—but a prepara-

tion for the good news about God? What is that disillusionment and frustration, that sense of the need of another and a greater power to come and take control—what is that, but God knocking at the door?

> Lord God of hosts, be with us yet,
> Lest we forget — lest we forget!

So in our own lives too. Life today is not particularly kind to the Christian values and the spiritual vision. There are thronging incessant cares and distractions that clamp us down to earth and crowd the angels out. But moments do come when something stirs within us—a memory perhaps of a mother's prayers from years of long ago, a glimpse of strange compelling beauty in the sky, some words of an old hymn, or perhaps it may be the sudden spectacle of glaring social injustice, some hateful wrong that demands a remedy, and with that, the nobler mood comes back and takes control. And what is that experience, but just God knocking at the door?

Robert Browning, with his profound spiritual perception, knew how impervious we human creatures can become to higher influence, how secure and settled in our materialist ways. But he noted also this, that

> Just when we are safest, there's a sunset-touch,
> A fancy from a flower-bell, some one's death,
> A chorus-ending from Euripides, —
> And that's enough for fifty hopes and fears
> As old and new at once as Nature's self
> To rap and knock and enter in our soul.

And what is that but God knocking at the door?

Carry the argument a stage further, and you come to this—even in the inmost citadel of self and sin no man is finally safe. There is conscience, there is remorse, there is the experience of encountering down the road of final apostasy the reproachful face of Jesus. There is the discovery that a man cannot sin and get away with it. And what is that discovery, that encounter, that remorse—but God knocking at the door?

You will remember a place where Shakespeare with over-whelming dramatic force drives this truth home. After Macbeth's dreadful deed was accomplished:

> Methought I heard a voice cry, Sleep no more!
> Macbeth doth murder sleep,—

and then suddenly, at the point of unbearable tension, comes the sound of knocking within:

> Whence is that knocking?
> How is't with me, when every noise appals me?
> What hands are here?

But it comes again and again and yet again until the man's nerves cannot stand it, and crying wildly:
Wake Duncan with thy knocking! I would thou couldst! he turns and rushes away.

Indeed Browning was right. "Just when we are safest, a sunset-touch—and that's enough." God raps and knocks and enters in the soul.

Today is the Lord's day, and we are gathered here in his House for worship. I do not know what worship ever means if it does not mean the eternal world signaling to us, beckoning to us, knocking at our door. For what God does in this act of worship is not only to withdraw us temporarily from the clamor and the turmoil of the world. It is to take the cross and the resurrection of Jesus and thrust them into the very center of our vision—that haunting, disturbing, challenging cross, that glorious, world-shattering, new-creating resurrection. And if there should be someone here who has been going through a lean and difficult time recently, with work and worry taking toll—losing interest in prayer and worship and the house of God, and feeling far off from spiritual things—nevertheless, you are here, and Christ is here, the cross on which he died for love of you is here, and the resurrection which makes him your living Contemporary is here. So it is that this hour's worship can be God knocking at the door.

"Behold, I stand at the door, and knock: *if any man hear my voice.*" So apparently it is not inevitable. If the man within hears —well and good. But if he does not, what then? I may know the mood of restlessness, a haunting dissatisfaction with the way my life has been going: but do I recognize that experience for what in fact it is, the voice of Christ to me? Or do I perhaps explain it away? "Oh, it is just weakness and sentiment, mere psychological suggestion." This is the question. When I am visited with compunction over the wrongs of society or the inner defeats of my own life, do I say to myself "You are a fool to worry"? Or do I say, "This is God. This is the Lord speaking to me in judgment and in mercy"?

For that is the truth. And it is precisely at this point that the Lord's day and the house of worship come to help us. They enable us to make a silence and a space within our crowded, jostled lives, so that the still small voice may have a chance and may reveal itself as the very voice of our Redeemer.

"Behold, I stand at the door, and knock: if any man hear my voice, *and open the door.*" So apparently that is not inevitable either. If the man within, having heard, chooses to open! But if he does not—what then? "I will not force the door," says Jesus. "I will not compel any man's allegiance. Until he chooses to open, I stand and wait."

Mark you, I am not saying anything at the moment about what may happen if the man inside wants to open, wants to be a disciple of this Christ and Master, and discovers that he cannot, finds that for one reason or another the door will just not move. That is different. I hope to say a word about that at the end. But the point just now is this: if the man does not wish to open, has no desire to be committed to discipleship, Christ will not break in. He stands and waits.

This is the sacredness of personality. Even God will not violate it. This is the mystery of free will.

Sometimes we almost wish that Christ would assert himself more forcibly. When you look out on the world and see how often the cause of truth is wrecked on the sheer hidebound inflexibility of stubborn men, God's plan turned down even when it is manifestly the one hope for the nations and the future of mankind, you may well feel like crying "Take action, Christ! Break down that door of dogged self-assertiveness and compel them to obey!"

But it is not Christ's way. Once—yes, once—he was tempted to try it. Once, early in his ministry, came the thought, "Shall I impose my will upon them? Shall I coerce belief? It will be in a good cause to win them for God and salvation." He saw how it could be done. The pinnacle of the temple! A sudden leap from there—the gasp of horror from the onlookers beneath—the shout of amazement at the spectacular miracle that would preserve his life! Surely that would batter down their unbelief and dazzle them into worship. That would burst open the door!

But he rejected it. He would not override man's freedom. He would not burgle the house of personality. They must come to him as sons, not slaves. "If any man open the door!"

Of course this lays an urgent responsibility on us. Here is this world in which we have to live, and here, embedded at the very heart of that world, are certain facts we call the Christian revelation—God incarnate, God in the sacrifice of the cross, God cleaving history asunder by the resurrection. The Christian revelation—this is the situation which urgently demands our response, the mighty act to which with our whole existence we have to say either yes or no. This is the measure of our responsibility.

In other words, if any man open the door, let him do it decisively, and not just a niggardly couple of inches. This was precisely the trouble here at Laodicea, the church to which the words were originally addressed, the community that was "neither cold nor hot," but politely, respectably tepid. Do not equivocate with God, is the message here. Do not muddle your logic and sell your intellectual integrity in that dubious way. Let it be either a plain decisive no, which can at least be understood, or else a ringing yes with all the passion of your being—not a few grudging inches, as when some grumpy, reluctant householder peers round the corner of the door when the bell is rung, glowering inhospitably and wishing you would begone. Not that. Fling wide the gate! It is the God of your life who is waiting.

Now look at this. We have had these two "ifs": "if any man hear my voice," "if any man open the door," neither of them inevitable. But now there follows, "If any man hear my voice and open the door, *I will come in.*" And this time it is inevitable. "I will come in, and sup with him." It is quite unconditional. And this is the humbling glory of the gospel.

There was once a big-hearted Roman soldier who asked Jesus to come and help him, for his servant was ill. But then second thoughts intervened. "Who am I to receive this Jesus into my house? I am not his kind—I am blunt and ordinary and unspiritual. The place is not fit to receive him. Lord, I am not worthy that thou shouldst come under my roof." And ever since that hour these words of his have been taken up in the confession of countless hearts:

> I am not worthy; cold and bare
> The lodging of my soul;
> How canst Thou deign to enter there?

Christ in my shabby, unspiritual life! If only I could have offered him a half-decent faith and hope and love! If only I had time to set the place to rights before he comes—though God knows it might take half a lifetime, there is so much to be done! But, friend, do you not remember? He was born in a stable. "Cold and bare the lodging of my soul." But not more cold and bare than that dark, drafty place at Bethlehem. And do you not remember again? There was a house in Jericho whose threshold no one would willingly cross, because it belonged to a squalid little renegade and traitor and collaborator, but Jesus went to supper with Zacchaeus. "If any man open the door—any man at all— I will come in and sup with him." The inevitability of grace!

Notice, further, the precise form of words—it is very significant. "I will sup with him, *and he with me.*" In other words, the positions are now reversed; the guest becomes the host. It is exactly what happened one night at Emmaus when two of them asked him in to share their meal. He took the bread and broke it for them, and in that instant they knew who he was. So when he comes into your life and mine. He may come as guest, but he remains as host. He means to take control.

Have you thought of that? Are you sure you would like it? To hand over the whole house—your whole self—to him? Get out the keys, the secret keys; will you give up every one to him? You had best think twice, declares the poet, before admitting even a human love into the placid stronghold of your life:

> If love should count you worthy, and should deign
> One day to seek your door and be your guest,
> Pause! ere you draw the bolt and bid him rest,
> If in your old content you would remain . . .
> He wakes desires you never may forget,
> He shows you stars you never saw before.

The whole sonnet might indeed have been written not about human love but about the Lord Jesus Christ. Has he not disturbed our dull, tedious contentment with desires which, once awakened, will haunt us till we die and stars we never saw before he came? It can be a mightily disturbing thing having Christ come in to take control.

> He makes you share with Him, for evermore,
> The burden of the world's divine regret.
> How wise you were to open not! and yet,
> How poor if you should turn Him from the door!

But I am conscious that someone may be saying to me, "You have not described my case. You have spoken of the man who will not open his heart to God, and you have spoken of the other who will—the defiant pagan and the faithful Christian. But I am different from both. I want to open, but the door refuses to move. The lock has grown rusty, and I cannot turn the key; the bolts are jammed, and I cannot pull them back. Even if Christ knocks till the house reverberates, I am not able to get that closed door open!"

CHRIST AT THE DOOR

131

Is that the trouble? The rust of prayerless days? The atrophy of faith, the dwindling of spiritual zest, the loss of spiritual power? You want the door to open, but it just will not budge— is that it?

Well, listen. We saw already that Christ never breaks down a door, if the owner does not want to have him in. He will not do it against a man's will. But this is quite different. Here is some- one who really wants to open the door and finds himself beaten. But is there not a story in the Gospels of a day when Christ came, "the doors being shut," and stood in the midst and said, "Peace be unto you"? Does that not give a sudden hint of how it might happen even now? Long ago in the Elizabethan age the poet-preacher of St. Paul's Cathedral, Dr. John Donne, had en- visaged this precise situation, of the door too firmly jammed to move, and he met it with a prayer:

> Batter my heart, three person'd God! for, You
> As yet but knock, breathe, shine, and seek to mend;
> That I may rise, and stand, o'erthrow me, and bend
> Your force, to break, blow, burn, and make me new . . .
> I am betroth'd unto Your enemy,
> Divorce me, untie, or break that knot again,
> Take me to You, imprison me, for I
> Except You enthrall me, never shall be free,
> Nor ever chaste, except You ravish me.

"Batter my heart, three person'd God!" And you can say, if not that, at least something like it. "Lord, here am I. I really want to let you in. But I have so little faith. I have forgotten how to pray. I am such an ordinary, unspiritual creature. I have tried to open the door but, Lord, there is the rust, the accumulated rust of years upon the bolts. You must do it for me. Break through! Smash that rusty lock. Batter my heart, three personed God! And even so—yes, even so—come, Lord Jesus!"

FACING OUR SKEPTICAL MOODS

*"I said, I will take heed to my ways, that I sin not with my tongue:
I will keep my mouth with a bridle . . . Lord, make me to know mine end,
and the measure of my days, what it is . . .
And now, Lord, what wait I for? My hope is in Thee . . .
I am a stranger with Thee, and a sojourner, as all my fathers were.
O spare me, that I may recover strength,
before I go hence, and be no more."*
PSALM 39:1-13

One effect the fierce strains and stresses of these critical days
ought to have is to drive the church and all of us back to the
psalms. Right down the centuries, to every succeeding generation the psalmists of Israel have spoken, but never surely did
their words ring out across the dark with more commanding
relevance than in our own confused and stormy day.

Let this Thirty-Ninth Psalm stand as an example. A word first
about its structure. It is a poem in four stanzas, the first three
stanzas having three verses each, the final stanza four. You
will observe that, as you pass from one stanza to the next, the
mood changes. The theme develops. The man's reaction to the
terrific pressure of life undergoes an exciting transformation.

I propose that we should travel this journey with him, step by
step. And I pray that it may be a real word of the Lord, this
psalm, to brace and rally us for our own pilgrimage in these
faith-testing days.

Take the first stanza—verses one to three. What is the keynote here? Put it in a word; it is "repression." Here you have
the conscious curbing and controlling of the skeptical mood.

The man is violently repressing a strong temptation to say

harsh and bitter things about life and providence. You can see him holding back, with a terrific effort, the wild, whirling words that would come pouring to his lips, "I said, I will take heed to my ways, that I sin not with my tongue. I will keep my mouth with a bridle," I will put a muzzle on my lips.

What was it that had roused the psalmist to such a pitch of feeling? It was the way the world was run. It was the sight of evil things so blatantly and jubilantly successful. "I will keep my mouth with a bridle, while the prosperity of the wicked is before me."

In other words, it was the eternal question which still sometimes comes beating down on us with the force of a tornado, Why does a good God stand it? Why are such devilries tolerated? Surely it ought to be possible for an omnipotent providence to keep its own house in order!

The psalmist was sorely tempted to give vent to such feelings in an outburst of radical cynicism. He was just on the point of letting himself go in a diatribe of scathing invective which would impeach the government of the universe.

But then suddenly, look, he rams on the brakes and calls a halt. Not a moment too soon, he represses the dangerous mood. "I said to myself, I will take heed to my ways, that I sin not with my tongue." Even if I feel like that, I must not say it in words. I must not let the denunciatory, vituperative mood out into speech. I will keep my mouth with a bridle!

Why did he impose that difficult decision? His own words make it clear. It was the sense that such wild talk was somehow spiritual treason. It was an inner chivalrous instinct telling him that under no circumstances must he say anything which might make things harder for others of God's believing children, many of whom were having a difficult enough time already without his depressing cynicism to make it worse. It was the consciousness that after all he, the psalmist, from his little corner of the world and with his dim finite mind, could see only an infinitesimal fraction of what God was doing, and that therefore for him to presume to impeach the universe would be preposterously naïve and arrogant and absurd. All that entered into it, when he applied the brake and checked the runaway words. "I will put a muzzle on my mouth!"

Now that example of his is worth pondering. Heaven knows that life is grim and perplexing enough for multitudes today without our indulging in depressing moods to make it harder. It is best to be quite blunt and frank about this. Any faithless talk about the divine ordering of the universe is treason to the saints.

The man who goes about saying "What a world this is! Just one gigantic muddle. If there is a 'divinity that shapes our ends,' it has botched and bungled the work" that man is doing what no soldier of Christ worthy of the name would ever dream of doing.

It is not only that he is spreading a blight of gloom and dejection when he ought rather to be rallying the courage in the depths of less valiant souls. It is also this—that he is disloyal to the good fight of faith, to all the heroic saints and martyrs who have fought that fight in ages past, and to the whole generation of the children of God who are fighting it today. He is deserting from faith's battlefield. He is setting his own moods and scruples and misgivings against the shining convictions for which Jesus vehemently laid down his life.

And there is still more. For after all, who is he, who is any man, yes, even the most intelligent member of the most brilliant brains trust that any television syndicate could bring together, to pronounce on the everlasting, inscrutable purposes of almighty God? As high as the heaven is above the earth, so far do God's vast designs outsoar the reach of our poor finite minds. We are no more qualified to comprehend the inner workings of God's purpose than the swallows nesting in the eaves of a church would be qualified to understand the purpose for which the church was built.

Far better, like the psalmist, take an oath of silence, before our agnostic moods and skeptical attitudes have an opportunity to indulge themselves. Better "take heed to our ways, and put a muzzle on our mouth, that we sin not with our tongue."

But now observe what happened here. The psalmist began to

find that his forcible repression of the skeptical mood was not an altogether satisfactory solution.

It never is. It is only a second-best. Indeed, the very act of repressing an emotion may have precisely the opposite effect to what was intended: it may simply drive that emotion down more deeply into the subconscious mind and fix it there more securely.

That is what the psalmist discovered. The muzzle on his mouth merely aggravated the trouble in his heart. "I was dumb," he writes, "with silence. But that only stirred my sorrow. My heart grew hot within me. While I was musing, the fire burned." While I was scrutinizing the problem, the smoldering sparks of my disquiet burst out into a blaze. The strategy of dumb silence, in spite of all his noble efforts, had broken down. Words had to come.

Now here we pass in the psalm from stanza one to stanza two—verses four to six. If the keynote of stanza one was repression, the repressing of the skeptical mood, the keynote here is *resolution,* the resolving of skepticism into prayer—just as in music we speak of the resolution of discords into harmony.

For notice this crucial thing: when this man's dangerous mood refused to be repressed and words had to come, the first words that came were a prayer. "Lord, make me to know my end."

That is the wonderful thing. Not the wild surge and thunder of scathing skepticism that a moment ago had seemed inevitable. Not the mocking, contemptuous laughter at life that would have proclaimed the disillusioned defeatist. No. What the man did with his wild, perilous background of doubt, perplexity, and misgiving was to turn it all into prayer. "Lord make me to know my end."

Is there not a vital principle here for all of us? When you and I are sore about life and perturbed by its grim confusions, don't let us say a word against it, until we have spoken first with God himself. That is the salutary rule. Turn it into prayer!

Too many of our prophets of radical gloom today have never thought of doing that. They go around spreading their vicious miasma of depression without ever daring to test their case in the secret place of the Most High, saying censorious things about God, behind God's back as it were, which they would never dream of saying to God's face.

Do you think that this psalmist, kneeling there in the presence of the Lord, could have said, "O God, I have come to tell you that I have found you out. Your vaunted gift of life is a cheat. Your world is incorrigible. Your promises derelict and worthless"? Do you think the psalmist, with all his inward doubts and grievances, could have prayed a thought like that? He might have thought it, and he might have said it, but could he have prayed it? The words would have frozen on his lips if he had tried. Well now, listen to this: any thought that will not fashion itself into prayer is a liar and deceiver. Any mood that resists the test of supplication has by that very fact proved its falsehood.

So I repeat that here is a most salutary rule: never a word against God until you have taken it first to God himself, until you have tried to say it looking full into those eyes of God which are Christ's eyes, until you have attempted to thrust your written indictment, your grievance and complaint, into the pierced and bleeding hands of Jesus. You will find you simply cannot do it then. There is no cure of the skeptical mood like the searching test of prayer.

Just watch what happened when the psalmist prayed. He suddenly perceived things in totally different perspective. He saw life steadily and whole, saw his immediate, obsessing problems against the background of eternity. In particular, he saw now the emptiness of the permissive freedom he had almost been inclined to envy, saw the utter hollowness of secularism's loud successes, saw the vanity and instability of glittering ramshackle civilizations that stubbornly flout the laws of the eternal. He sets this down bluntly in verse six: "Surely these men walk in a vain show. They heap up riches, and know not who shall gather them." It is almost a forecast of one of Jesus' most devastating comments on the secular cupidity of an affluent society, "Thou fool, this night thy soul shall be required of thee."

Here we pass in the psalm from stanza two to stanza three—verses seven to nine. If the keynotes of stanzas one and two were repression and resolution—the repressing of the skeptical mood, and the resolving of skepticism into prayer—the keynote here is *realization*: the realizing of the one thing needful.

The psalmist suddenly becomes piercingly aware that in this difficult and desperate world there is after all just one thing which finally matters: to possess God. Look at his words. "And now, Lord, what wait I for?" Why need I wait at all? "My hope is in thee."

This realization, for those who really come awake to it, is the most liberating and illuminating experience in the world. It extricates from disillusionment and despair. "My windows are all darkened," wrote George Macdonald of a troubled period in his life, "all save the sky-light." What the psalmist is telling me is that I don't need to wait till my problems are solved and life's vexed questions settled; as long as I have God, I have everything that matters. I don't need to wait till I can explain the universe or give a satisfactory answer in terms of logic and theory to its baffling enigmas; it is not an explanation nor a theory I am needing, it is a reinforcing Presence and if I have that, I can march on now, without waiting, devoid of fear.

In order to live the victorious life, I don't need to wait till my disabling handicaps are eliminated or the thorn in the flesh removed. In order to run the straight race, I don't need to wait till the road emerges from the rough places and the shadows into the open and the sunshine. Now, today, this very moment—amid the thronging cares and anxieties that beset me—I can go with the step of a conqueror, if I have God at my right hand.

Yes, there is something even greater, namely this—I don't need to wait, when my sinful heart is yearning for the blessedness of being forgiven and ransomed and set free, I don't need to wait until I have done penance for my sins, don't need to wait until the hour seems more propitious and I have fashioned something like a decent character to offer to the Lord. If I have once seen God as he comes to meet me at the cross of Jesus, then I can cry—with far more assurance than any psalmist—"Now,

Lord, what wait I for? What can I possibly wait for after this? My hope, my certainty, are in thee!" I know this is the one thing needful in this dark, stormy world—to possess the living God revealed in Christ, the same yesterday, today, and for ever.

When the psalmist, having reached his saving realization, goes on to add, I was dumb, I opened not my mouth, because thou didst it," it is a very different kind of silence from the muzzled taciturnity we saw him struggling to achieve in his first stanza. There it was the strained, uneasy silence of forcible repression. But he is far beyond that now. This is the evangelical silence of acceptance of the will of God.

But let there be no misunderstanding. I am not extolling a pious resignation that lies down before the glaring ills of life and weakly tolerates them as if they were inevitable; there is no virtue in that. But I am remembering One greater than the psalmist of whom it stands written, "He was oppressed, and he was afflicted; yet he opened not his mouth. As a sheep before her shearers is dumb, so he openeth not his mouth." Anyone who suggests there was weakness in that silence does not know what he is talking about. It was the strong silence of entire devotion to the will of God. "I opened not my mouth, because thou didst it."

Do you see what this means for you and me? Surely this. If we can see God's hand in our experience; if, however daunting the road, there shines for us, as there shone for Jesus on the Via Dolorosa, the high conviction "This is the path on which God means my feet to be"; if even dimly and from afar we have caught some glimmer of the meaning of that quiet, amazing saying with which Christ turned to face the cross, "The cup which my Father gives me, shall I not drink it?" then we are on the way to learn the tremendous truth that for those who give their lives over vehemently and heartily to the divine control, saying amen to God's will for them, there can be in this world no irreparable disasters, no deepest ills that cannot yield overwhelming good, no thorns that cannot be woven into a crown.

And this brings us to the end, to the note on which the psalmist closes, in his fourth and final stanza—verses ten to thirteen. We have heard in the earlier stanzas the notes of repression, resolution, realization. Here the note is *recapturing*—the recapturing of the pilgrim spirit.

His words towards the end are like the drumbeat of a pilgrim march. "I am a stranger with thee, and a sojourner, as all my fathers were." Here I have no continuing city. Here I am a resident alien, with a temporary lodging at best, and no sure hold on life, a restless wanderer, never absolutely at home, always journeying on, and knowing full well that, when I die, the world will still be pursuing its accustomed way, quite oblivious that for a brief span I have made my sojourn here.

It speaks volumes for the psalmist's faith that though his knowledge of a future beyond the grave was clouded and uncertain, although he can only end with those most poignant words about "going hence and being no more," he nevertheless casts himself without one shadow of doubt upon the God who sees the end from the beginning. "I am a stranger, an alien and a sojourner, but at least I am a sojourner *with thee*. I am God's pilgrim. And God will call me home!"

The recapturing of the pilgrim spirit—do we not need that today, in this secularized, mechanized age which tends to have no time for the world unseen and the beckoning horizons of eternity, and very little but contempt for the homesickness of the exiled spirit that once induced the apostolic cry "I have a desire to depart and to be with Christ, which is far better"? The temper of the age in a predominantly materialistic society like ours can be terribly tyrannical, imposing its this-worldly standards of success and satisfaction, making totalitarian demands on mind and emotion, hope and desire, and branding all talk of being born again into another dimension of life as pious, fraudulent fantasy. But if Augustine was right when he cried, "O God, thou hast made us for thyself, and our heart is restless till it rests in thee"; if the Bible is right when it says "Thou hast set eternity in their hearts," then the secular utopianism of today is the craziest of philosophies. Yes, and any world view or theology or church which plays down the pilgrim note and tries to domesticate us firmly in this present world is distorting the basic reality of existence and perpetrating a treason on the gospel.

It is precisely the recapturing of the pilgrim spirit which is offered us in Christ. We Christians, far more than any psalmist, can hold with confidence the faith in a world beyond this sphere of sense and time. For in the Word made flesh at Bethlehem we have been given the clue to life and destiny. We have seen the age to come and the dimension of eternity breaking through into our categories of space and time and refashioning history before our eyes. To us there has come, like the sound of ten thousand trumpets, a great Voice crying athwart the ages: "Fear not! I am the first and the last; I am he that liveth, and was dead, and behold I am alive for evermore—the firstborn of a great brotherhood, the resurrection and the life!"

And so, recapturing the pilgrim spirit, we turn to the road again, with Christ's dear voice to cheer us on, his presence to gladden all the way, and his power prevailing not only to bring the exile home but also to make even the castaways and the outlaws of this earth into citizens of heaven.

There was a day when a group of early Christians were being martyred in the Roman colosseum for the faith of Christ. As the shadows of the last agony came down upon them, the watching thousands heard from that arena of death a sudden loud triumphant shout, and it was this, "We have lived and we have loved, and we shall live and we shall love again. Hallelujah!" Valiant faith! Ours be that shining confidence. We have lived and loved. We shall live and love again!

Aliens? Yes. Strangers, sojourners, pilgrims? Yes. But "sojourners," as the psalm says, *with thee,* with God, the living God who in Christ has brought life and immortality to light, the strength and stay of every pilgrim road, the guarantee of the most wonderful homecoming at the end, when the dim glimpses of eternity which we have on earth are merged into full and perfect vision.

I know that safe with Him remains,
Protracted by His power,
What I've committed to His trust,
Till the decisive hour.

Then, the morning and the King's face, to whom be the glory for ever.

KING FOR EVER

142

THE POWER
OF HIS RESURRECTION

"Now the God of peace, that brought again from the dead our Lord Jesus,
that great Shepherd of the sheep,
through the blood of the everlasting covenant,
make you perfect in every good work to do His will,
working in you that which is wellpleasing in His sight,
through Jesus Christ;
to whom be glory for ever and ever. Amen."
HEBREWS 13:20, 21

Perfect? in every good work? To do his will? But surely, knowing myself as I do, knowing something of the world in which I have to live, this is a preposterous ideal, an absurd heightening of much more ordinary, pedestrian ambitions. I want something humanly attainable. If I can make even a half-decent showing in the fight for character, if I can be sure of seeing the pilgrimage through without weakness or dishonor, I shall be quite content. That is good enough for me. Perfect? In every good work, to do his will? It is a dream, remote, fantastic, out of reach for ever!

This reaction is understandable. Its logic, humanly speaking, is impeccable. Its healthy humility is commendable.

But before we accept it as final or inevitable, let us have another look at what the apostle is saying. In particular, let us look at the context in which these words about being perfect in every good work are set. He begins with God, and not just with some undefined idea of God, but with God in one particular aspect. He begins with the God of the resurrection. Now this is absolutely vital to his argument. It changes the whole perspective. "The God who brought again from the dead the Lord Jesus, make you perfect."

So let us try beginning there also. Before we start arguing about what is possible or not possible in the Christian life, let us get our standpoint right.

The most characteristic word of the Christian religion is the word "resurrection." If you had to choose one word to gather up and focus and express the very essence of the New Testament faith, this would have to be your choice. This, in fact, according to the Bible is what Christianity essentially is—a religion of resurrection. This is what every worshiping congregation is intended in the purpose of God to be—a community of the resurrection. And this is what the gospel offers today to this dark and ruined world, where men peering into the future are daunted by the well-nigh impossible task of creating order out of chaos and life out of death—the power of the resurrection. When I had the task of teaching the New Testament at New College in Edinburgh, my closest colleague was that fine scholar-saint of beloved memory, Professor William Manson. One sentence constantly on Manson's lips was this, "The only God the New Testament knows is the God of the resurrection." In short, this is the essential evangel. Rejoice that the Lord is arisen!

It is true, of course, that for us Christians the cross must ever stand at the very heart of things. If I, with my bungling, sinful nature, lose sight of the cross even for a day, I am done for, and I know it. But I may gaze at the cross and miss the gospel that saves, for I am still on the wrong side of Easter. This is Christianity's symbol, not the dead figure of the crucifix, but Christ risen, trampling a broken cross beneath his feet—"neither is there salvation in any other."

Far too often we have regarded the resurrection as an epilogue to the gospel, an addendum to the scheme of salvation, a codicil to the divine last will and testament—thereby falsifying disastrously the whole emphasis of the Bible. The fact is there would never have been a New Testament at all, apart from the burning certainty of all its writers that he whose mighty deeds they were recording had conquered death and was alive for ever. Apart from this fact, we should not be meeting here today, this church, like every other, is built on the foundation of the resurrection. For this fact was no mere appendix to the faith, this was, this is, the faith—the overpowering, magnificent good news. And the men who first told of it were certain there was no darkness it could not illuminate, no despair it would not smite with sudden hope. This is the only gospel the New Testament knows. Rejoice that the Lord is arisen!

It is important to observe just how this writer to the Hebrews expresses it. He says of the resurrection, agreeing in this with all the other New Testament writers, "It was God who did this thing. It was God's mighty act that brought up from the dead the Lord Jesus."

This emphasis is characteristic and vital. It is immensely significant that those first Christians never preached the resurrection simply as Jesus' escape from the grave, the reanimation of One who had died, the return of the Master to his friends. They always proclaimed it as the living God in omnipotent action. It was God's hands that had taken the stone which the builders rejected and made it the head of the corner. "This is the Lord's doing," they declared, "and it is marvelous in our eyes."

In other words, their insight taught them that it is what lies behind the resurrection that matters, not the actual method of its occurrence—which is a mystery about which you can debate unendingly—but what lies behind it. And what lies behind it is this, God vindicating the dreams for which Christ died, God ratifying righteousness, justice, and truth against the evil powers that hate these things and seek to crush and crucify them, God announcing his invincible divine determination to make Christ lord of all.

I heard a man recently on the radio arguing that Christianity has had its day and claiming to prove from statistics that the church is facing gradual decline and ultimate extinction, and he proceeded to pronounce its obituary. And I wanted to cry, "Man, don't you know that God is alive, the God who creates and recreates, and who will never allow his word to return to him void?"

It is at this point that the resurrection fact strikes right into world history as it confronts us today. This is the dramatic relevance of Easter to our own confused, bewildered age. Many in these tense, tumultuous days are trembling for the ark of God. Look at the endemic conflicts between nations, the eruption of violence and cruelty and hatred, the appearance of sinister new brands of lawlessness and terrorism, the false values of a sick society, the domineering sway of ideologies which make a mock of freedom and true humanity. It is not surprising that many are haunted by the fear that the powers of darkness may ultimately win the battles, paralyzed by that terrible doubt. But listen! What if God has already taken the measure of the evil forces at their very worst and most malignant, has met the challenge precisely at that point, routing the darkness and settling the issue? This is the conviction that makes the New Testament—which, mark you, was written in a far grimmer age than ours—at once the most exciting and the most relevant book in the world. This is indeed the basic fact of our holy faith. The power that was strong enough to get Jesus out of the grave, and thus to set going the whole Christian movement across the centuries, mighty enough to shatter and confound the hideous demonic alliance of evil, creative enough to smite death with resurrection—this power is in action still. What are we doing in this church today if what I am saying is not true? Simply nursing an illusory hope. But no, it is not that. We are celebrating a magnificent incontrovertible reality. And therefore you and I, amid all the battering dilemmas and disillusionments of contemporary history, can lift up our heads, knowing and rejoicing that God still reigns, and that God is in the field when he is most invisible. Having accomplished this mighty act in Christ, he shall not fail nor be discouraged until he has consummated his eternal purpose and brought in the kingdom of heaven.

But this confident outlook on history is not the whole truth of the matter. There is also a much more intimate and personal implication affecting you and me right now. And it is this which the writer to the Hebrews fixes on in that prayer which might otherwise seem so impossible and fantastic. "May the God of peace, who brought up from the dead our Lord Jesus, make you perfect." That is to say, the same divine creative energy which resurrected Christ and started the greatest movement in history is available for you, for me—and this, mark you, not only at death to raise us up, but here and now to help us to live.

Who can realize this and not be thrilled by it? Here is this man praying for those Christians and for that church, that the identical force which God had exerted in taking Jesus out of the grave might now operate creatively in their own lives, that this same energy might go inwardly to work to make them strong and whole and brave and vital—to make them, in short, resurrected personalities, throbbing with new life!

I sometimes wonder, have we ever really comprehended that this, nothing less, is what the gospel is about, the gospel we so often take with a shockingly matter-of-fact casualness? Here is the offer: the power which shattered death for Jesus, the power in which Christ is alive at this moment, to help us now to live!

Certainly it is this that explains the immense verve of early Christianity. They went, those followers of Jesus, to men who had been defeated—physically, morally, and spiritually defeated scores, hundreds of times—and they said, "Here is a way of victory! God has brought again from the dead the Lord Jesus. With such a power at work, what may not happen—for you?"

That was the message. And lest any of their hearers should think they were being merely rhetorical and romantic, always these men of the New Testament could go on to say, "We know it, for we have proved it. It has worked for us."

Actually, it was not necessary for them to say it. For the fact itself was apparent. The resurrection does not depend for its credibility on verbal statements. How was it that some ordinary, fallible, blundering men were able to go out and turn the world upside down? It was not that they were commanding personalities—most of them were not. It was not that they had official backing, impressive credentials, illustrious patronage; of all that they had less than nothing. It was this—that they had clearly established contact with the power that had resurrected Jesus, or rather, that this supercharged power had laid hold of them. And still today they accost us, saying, "It is abroad now in the earth, the power of the resurrection. Why not for you?" And they look at us with absolute assurance, "Why not for you?" "Oh," we retort to them, "you are being emotional now. Did you not know we had domesticated all that kind of thing long ago, unburdening our minds of the incubus of the unaccountable and eliminating the dimension of the miraculous from our creed?"

We are so slow to take it in. "Our lives," we say, "are not the stuff out of which God's Easter victories are made. And as for hoping to live on Christ's level, with that new risen quality of life, why, what's the use? Our problems are too many, our thwarting frailties too baffling, our chains of defeat too firmly shackled on our souls. We have toiled all night and taken nothing."

In this respect, we are like our forefathers who lived all their days in a world containing the marvel of electricity and never guessed it was there. Or we are like the man with the rake in Bunyan's dream, gazing permanently downwards, so obsessed with his task of gathering the sticks and straws and dust off the floor that he never noticed, standing behind him, a shining figure with a celestial crown held forth in his hand. We are so apt to be obsessed with the sticks and straws of our own weak efforts of will, ineffectual resolves, and insubstantial longings: never dreaming that the Lord God who resurrected Christ is standing there beside us, with that gift of supernatural power—ours, if we would but take it!

But those men of the New Testament refuse to be daunted by such recreant, unbelieving moods. "Do you not believe," they ask us, "in God the Father Almighty, maker of heaven and earth, through whose creative Spirit all things are possible?" Paul in one shining passage spells out for the Ephesians the scale on which God proposes to go to work in their lives, the measure of the resources available to them; he says it is "on the scale of the might which God exerted when he raised Christ from the dead." And if what Paul and this writer to the Hebrews are saying is true—and who am I, who is anyone, to deny it? how irrational our doubts and fears become! "The God who brought again from the dead the Lord Jesus, shall he not—today if you will ask him—revive and quicken you?"

But there is one thing that remains to be added. For there is one essential condition to be fulfilled before the God of the resurrection can thus come creatively into your life and mine. If this dynamic reality with its healing properties is to lay hold of us, if our spirits are to know the baptism of power and the dimension of eternity, one thing is needful. Self-surrender. Self-commitment.

This writer to the Hebrews has very dramatically reminded us of that. For did you notice that even this magnificent verse has something like a streak of blood across it? Did you hear, through this shout of Easter praise and the trumpets of victory, the diapason note of sacrifice? "The God of peace, who brought again from the dead our Lord Jesus, *through the blood of the everlasting covenant.*" There was no road to Easter for Jesus except by Good Friday, no way to that risen eternal quality of life except by life laid down. And that being so, this too is axiomatic: there can be no road to the power of Easter for any of us except at the cost of self-commitment; no way to the experience of having God's energies loosed and set free into our life except through the discipline of self-surrender. That is the condition.

Here, then, is the question I must face, and you, and all of us. With this supernatural force available—the same power that resurrected Christ and energized the church and that has made life new for multitudes—why should my life ever be helpless and maimed and impoverished and defeated? Is it that I have been unwilling to travel the road that Jesus went and all the saints—the exacting road of consecration?

The ultimate secret of resurrection power was given by William Cowper in lines we often sing:

> The dearest idol I have known,
> Whate'er that idol be,
> Help me to tear it from Thy throne,
> And worship only Thee.

That is the streak of blood. Tear it from thy throne and worship only thee. That is the Good Friday sacrifice. And beyond it, the power of a new Easter—the marvel of life blossoming red from the dust of self's defeat, the joy and peace of triumphing in Christ here on earth and of knowing that this is but a foretaste and a first installment of something still more wonderful to come when we are finally made one with him for ever.

For this is what lies beyond the horizon of our pilgrimage. The Christ of the resurrection is the firstborn of a great brotherhood. Hints and anticipation of it are indeed not lacking here. Especially when a congregation gathers in the house of God for worship, one becomes vividly aware of the communion of saints and the cloud of witnesses, those who once sojourned and worshiped with us here and are now for ever with the Lord. When a congregation has existed for many years and generations, by far the greater part of its fellowship comes to be beyond the river; almost everyone can think of dear ones yonder on the immortal side of death. They are with Christ, numbered with his saints in glory everlasting.

Our destiny—if indeed we are united to the living Christ here and now, and if we are thus through him joined to the immortality of God (and this is what I have been pleading for)—our destiny is to be reunited one day with those loved ones in the habitations of his glory and dominion, never, never to part again. And all guaranteed to us by the Christ of Easter and by the risen life he is offering us now. To him be the glory and the thanksgiving this day and for ever. Jesus, still lead on!

"I COMMEND YOU TO GOD"

*"And now I commend you to God and to the word of His grace,
which is able to build you up and to give you the inheritance
among all those who are sanctified."*
ACTS 20:32 (RSV)

A congregation assembled for worship is an event of a very
special kind. There is no other gathering in the world quite
like it. What constitutes its difference is nothing visible or cal-
culable. Indeed, it may look ordinary and commonplace enough.
But the reality is extraordinary and unique.

For what brings a congregation together is something which,
though it permeates life and the world, is also at the same time
right out of this world. It is the mystery of the eternal. It is
the orientation of mind and heart towards the source and origin
of all existence. It is the fact that here we stand on the boundary
line between the visible and the invisible, and have communion
with the One in whom we live and move and have our being.

Not that everyone in a congregation is necessarily aware of
this. Not that this basic motive for churchgoing is always recog-
nizable and articulate. It may quite well be that in a gathered
congregation there are those who do not know why they are there
at all. Habit, perhaps? A sense of duty? A brief hour's escape
from household or business cares? Some respite from the noise
and tumult of the world? The pressure perhaps of the question
whether it is really true, the faith which the church reputedly
stands for? Can it indeed be true in the vastly changed world in
which we have to live today? Yes, there is a whole medley of
intermingling motives.

But down beneath all that there is something deeper. There

is something that differentiates a congregation at worship from any other gathering. There is the commerce of the finite with the infinite. There is the mystery of an all-encompassing Presence. There is the feeling after God.

How can one speak to such a situation? If one had only one thing to say and only one chance to say it, what would it have to be? This is where I find the words of our text so vividly relevant. They come leaping right out of the page to meet and challenge us.

Here was Paul on his last journey to Jerusalem. He would have preferred to stay where he was, with his young eager churches of the West. But it was no use: there was Another Will, inscrutable and irresistible, leading him away, and it would never let him go back anymore. "Now, behold, I go bound in the Spirit to Jerusalem, not knowing the things that shall befall me there."

He had been visiting all the old places for the last time— Thessalonica, Berea, Philippi, Corinth, scenes of his ministry, each with associations that kept tugging at his heart and memories that would never fade. He had been reliving the great hours spent in each, meeting old friends and sharing old memories. And now, "bound in the Spirit to Jerusalem."

The ship came in sight of Miletus, close to Ephesus, and put in to land. And Paul decided he must have one last talk with his friends of Ephesus nearby. He had lived a long time with that Ephesian church, and nowhere had life for him been fuller or more strenuous. And now the time was short; the ship was due to sail again quite soon, but he would have one last talk with those folk with whom he had lived and labored and to whom he knew he would never go back—just a few parting words.

Here they stand in the twentieth chapter of Acts. It is not a brilliant piece of art and oratory. It was not delivered to a vast congregation or a crowded general assembly, only to a little handful of people. It is very quiet and simple and confiding. It is not Paul the dialectician, the controversialist, the theologian, the master of massive argument. But it is one of the most inexpressibly moving things in the Bible. He recalls their intimate and precious fellowship together in Christian work and worship, dwells for a moment on the gospel he had tried to preach— "repentance towards God and faith towards Jesus Christ"—turns to glance at the unknown path he is entering on, tells them frankly of his premonition that this visit to Jerusalem will be the end and that he will not be returning to Ephesus nor ever meeting those friends of his on earth again, calls God to witness he has loved their souls with passion and sought to share with them the secrets of the Lord, vows they will ever be in his heart to live and die with him. "And now," he adds, for even last words must come to an end and tongues must cease, "now I commend you to God and to the word of his grace, which is able to build you up and to give you the inheritance among all those who are sanctified."

Will you ponder that? Surely there is something here for us today.

Paul looks at those dear Ephesian friends of his with whom he has shared so much, and he says this first, "*I commend you to God.*"

You see, what takes a miscellaneous group of people and welds them into that marvelous thing, the fellowship of a Christian congregation, is not any human factor, Paul, Apollos, Cephas, or any of them; it is God the Holy Ghost. It is the electricity of the supernatural in the midst. That is what makes the church—in spite of all its critics and detractors—a fellowship with which there is nothing else on earth you can compare.

"Who are Paul, Apollos, Cephas?" wrote the apostle once to the Corinthians. "They are only voices; they know in part and prophesy in part and then pass back into the silence again. But God abides, God endures unchanging on and gives the increase." Therefore, said Paul, leaving this dear flock of Ephesus, "I commend you to God!"

There was a fine thing John Wesley wrote in a letter to a pastor at the end of a long ministry. "Be of good cheer! He who took care of the sheep before you were born will not forget them when you are dead."

Today there is a constant stream of talk about so-called gaps in the life and witness of the church—the generation gap, the communications gap, the culture gap, the credibility gap. But there is one fact that bridges them all, one focus that gathers all the diversity into one. In such a gathering as this, there are some who have grown old in the faith and may not have many more earthly miles to travel; I commend you to God. There are young men and women, gazing down the untrodden years and wondering what lies waiting there: I commend you to God. There are those to whom the changing scenes of life have brought great joy or crushing sorrow: I commend you to God. There are those who have found the road of faith hedged round with doubts and difficulties, who do not know perhaps why their steps should ever lead into any house of prayer: I commend you to God.

Charles Wesley in his day wished he had a thousand tongues to tell the gospel forth, but even a thousand tongues would leave so immeasurably much unsaid the half would not be told, no, nor the thousandth part of the transcendent reality. But one thing abides, better than anything else in the world: and Paul knew and realized it when, looking on those dear friends of his at Ephesus, he said quite simply, "I commend you to God."

"And," he went on, "to the word of his grace—I commend you *to the Word!*"

That means, of course, the totality of divine revelation. But for us in a very special sense it means Holy Scripture, this marvelous book which is the very life of the church.

I am sure the preacher's task today is not to propound theories and opinions, certainly not to use isolated texts as pegs for his own views and arguments; it is to take this book and let it speak for itself. For the real question which this confused, bewildered generation is flinging at the church today is the identical question which they flung at Jeremiah long ago, "Is there any word *from the Lord?*" And Jeremiah answered, "There is."

And so I hope you will go on exploring this book and drawing on its riches to the journey's end. Surely it is one of the deepening amazements of life—the perennial freshness of this book of God. Isaac Newton said that after all his scientific discoveries he felt still just like a child playing with pebbles on the shore, while the great ocean of truth lay undiscovered before him. That is how any of us may well feel about the Bible. "In the Bible," said Coleridge, "there is more than *finds* me than in all other books put together: the words of the Bible find me at greater depths of my being."

All the drama of life is here, all the joy and sorrow of the world, all your own hopes and fears and moods that batter and besiege the soul. It never grows stale. It never leaves you in the lurch. It will never fail to meet you with help and healing and supernatural reinforcement. "I commend you to God—and to the Word!"

Further, Paul adds, "I commend you to the word *of his grace.*" That word "grace" is the very key word of the gospel. And Paul was determined not to let this final hour with his Ephesians pass without making one more declaration of the relevance and validity and all-sufficiency of the grace of God.

In these days we are busily concerned to reduce the great words of our religion into modern speech. We have almost made a fetish of getting our language contemporary—with the idea that the old hallowed words cannot be relevant unless they are made colloquial and matter of fact. I wonder if there may not be a way of trying to update the gospel which simply results in denuding it of the mysterious and supernatural and thereby robbing it of its inherent power. At any rate, where this word "grace" is concerned, I would say it is a risky business trying to reduce such a word.

For what does grace mean throughout the Bible? Certainly nothing vague and general like favor or helpfulness or philanthropy. It means two quite specific things about the divine love—on the one hand, that that love always *takes the initiative,* goes into action first, and on the other, that it does this *for the undeserving.* Always where the word occurs these two facts are present—God taking the first step in reconciliation and doing it for those who have no merit to show.

You and I know full well where Paul discovered that. It was at the gates of Damascus. From the hour of his conversion, it was these two facts that filled his thoughts and fired his imagination and became the motive and the mainspring and the master-passion of his apostleship. He would never have been in this thing at all if God on that day had not taken the initiative and acted first and done it for the least deserving, most rebellious of his creatures. After *that,* "Necessity is laid upon me," was his cry, "woe is me if I preach not the gospel," and commend you to his grace!

Never forget the twofold meaning of that word; write it on your heart today—God's initiative, for the undeserving.

Do you not see that the one hope for this broken world lies there, that the only way out of the mad, vicious circle of suspicion and fear and hatred and war, and hatred and fear and suspicion and war again, on and on for ever, the only way out of that permanent predicament of the human race bound to the inexorably revolving wheel, is in the fact that God takes the initiative, offers a new beginning, and does it for folk without an atom or a shred of merit and deserving?

And do you not see that the life and health and peace of your own soul lie there?

Here is a gospel that shatters all human righteousness, makes havoc of all aloof superior pretensions, and shames us for feeling better than other people and criticizing them because we felt like that—a gospel that says "You can't earn a citizenship in Zion, not ever! You can't ever merit salvation. Take it for nothing, or not at all!"

That is grace—God's initiative in Christ, offered freely to the undeserving. "*While we were yet sinners,* he died." And today once again I press this gospel upon you. "I commend you to his grace."

Then Paul goes on, *"which is able* to build you up." It is one of the great recurring watchwords of the New Testament—"He is able!" "The grace of God is able!" It rings out like a trumpet from page after page, "Christ is able!"

That is why the early church, in spite of all its human weakness, throbbed with that sense of energy, exhilaration, and vitality which makes the New Testament the most exciting book in the world. When the men of the early church preached Christ, they preached him as One who was alive and regnant, able in the power of his resurrection to flood the dark places of the world with light, able to shake the Roman Empire and to change the face of history, able to make the crooked straight, the weak strong, the defeated irresistible. And they were not romancing when they talked like that. Their own eyes had seen it happening—it had indeed happened to them—and they *knew.*

> He comes the prisoners to relieve
> In Satan's bondage held;
> The gates of brass before Him burst,
> The iron fetters yield.

So I am going to say this to you today: Never become so obsessed with the problems of the world and the perplexities of your own life that you forget the glorious overplus of power of Christ your Savior. He is risen and alive and able today—for this poor broken shambles of an earth and for our own personal needs and longings—"to do exceeding abundantly above what we ask or think."

That distinguished missionary Stanley Jones—who gave us a book which in its day became a classic, *The Christ of the Indian Road*—has told how in his early days in India he was prostrated with illness and depression. One day in Lucknow he turned into a church to pray; and there he heard a voice saying "Are you ready for the work to which I have called you?" "No, Lord," he replied, "I'm done for. I've reached the end of my resources, and I can't go on." Then said the voice, "If you will turn the problem over to me and not worry about it, I will take care of it." "Lord," came the eager reply, "I close the bargain right here." And when he rose from his knees he knew that he was healed, possessed with life and hope and peace. "He is able!"

And what of the church? Do you ever ask yourself how in all the world the church that began in an upper room long ago and far away has survived to this hour? How in the name of all that is wonderful has it not been smashed by the tornado of the Herods and the Caesars and the principalities and powers? Why has not the burning bush been utterly consumed? It is because in the midst of the church there has stood and stands today the risen and regnant Lord.

It is this—not the frills of life and religion, but this central affirmation—that is the very keystone of the faith: Jesus risen and alive, the Lord of history and the Savior of mankind. Our very presence here today is proof of it. "He is able!"

Now watch how the apostle continues: "He is able *to build you up*." That means—to lead you on from strength to strength, from vision to vision, from discovery to discovery.

Paul, speaking thus to this nucleus of an Ephesian church, is speaking still to the whole church everywhere. The church, thank God, has had its wonderful days of flood tide and revival. But we are not going to be content with a dead memory. "Speak unto the children of Israel *that they go forward!*" Good and great as the revival years have been, there are better and greater coming. God speed you to the next milestone and beyond! "In him we live, *and move,* and have our being." And it does not matter if you do not see the road, as long as you see the star.

So in our own lives too. "Able to build you up" in your personal religious life, to show you (as long ago Brendan put it) "wonder upon wonder, and every wonder true." You ought to be seeing far more in the gospel today than when it first commanded your allegiance: you ought to go on seeing more and more in it to the end of the road. In his seventy-seventh year Corot the painter remarked, "If the Lord lets me live two years longer, I think I can paint something beautiful." Always that reaching out to something beyond! When David Livingstone was found dead on his knees in Central Africa, his diary was open before him, and the last entry was, "My Jesus, my Savior, my life, my all, anew I dedicate myself to thee." New discoveries and dedications right on to the end!

There is no room in Christianity for the arrested development of the soul which thinks it has found everything and settles down content in spiritual rigidity and petrification. He is able to keep building you up, from strength to strength, from character to character, from glory to glory—until at last his new creation is complete.

So we reach the final word of Paul's message to those friends he would never see again, "And to give you the inheritance among all those who are sanctified."

You see, his thought is soaring now far away beyond Ephesus, Miletus, Jerusalem, Rome, and all the tears and partings of this world—away to the church in heaven, and to the eternal Home where they would all meet at last. The sands of time were fast running out for the apostle, and the irreversible years were carrying him away. It is at such a time that the realization of the swift approach of journey's end can fill the human heart with regret for vanished possibilities, and with a longing for the days that are no more. Robert Louis Stevenson once struck that note:

> The eternal dawn, beyond a doubt,
> Shall break o'er hill and plain,
> And put all stars and candles out
> Ere we be young again.

But Paul's attitude is different. In anticipation, he is away beyond even the sands of time now. He is away in the church invisible, where God's redeemed—the multitude which no man can number—sing forth the glory of their Redeemer. This, he tells the Ephesians, is your inheritance.

We are moving on to that; we are walking on the borderland of that, and, said Richard Baxter so memorably, looking up into the face of Jesus—

"I COMMEND YOU TO GOD"

If Thy work on earth be sweet,
What will Thy glory be?

Do you ever wonder what the saints speak about to one another when they meet in glory? I think I can guess one theme at least, the story of one encounter in varied forms. I think that Paul, meeting friends in heaven, would speak about the road to Damascus, and the woman of Samaria about Jacob's well, and Peter about the fishing boat on his highland loch, and Zacchaeus about the sycamore tree, and Thomas about the upper room—always remembering "There God met me! There I was apprehended by Christ." And perhaps one day up yonder this very church where we are gathered now, this dear House of God, may be mentioned, and one will say to another, "It was there I found the light. It was there I gave my heart to Christ!"

"He is able to give you the inheritance among all those who are sanctified," incorruptible, undefiled, and that fadeth not away.

Too good to be true? Too incredible to be real? An impossible prospect surely for ordinary sin-stained creatures like ourselves?

Rabbi Duncan once thought so. He was one of the saints of his generation. But, "If there is anything," he said, "in which I would be inclined to contradict him, it would be if I heard him say, 'Well done, good and faithful servant.'" I can understand that. And so can you. We have not given him a fraction of the love and service we could have given. And yet it stands, the promised inheritance, defying all the logic of human regrets and failures; it stands, the miracle to crown all miracles, with Christ's own promise to guarantee it. "Enter into the joy of your Lord!" The One who spoke these words is here today. I know he is present now. I see the light of the glory of God upon his face. I hear the cadences of his dear voice, proclaiming, "Come, ye blessed of my Father, inherit the kingdom!" And I beg you, all of you with one heart and mind and spirit, to cry, "So be it, Christ! Lead on for ever! Through life and death we follow thee—and beyond death, into glory."